OPTIONS TRADING FOR BEGINNERS

A COMPLETE CRASH COURSE TO
GET TO KNOW ALL YOU NEED
ABOUT INVESTING STRATEGIES
AND HOW TO MAKE PROFIT
FOR A LIVING WITH TRADING
OPTIONS

JOE DOUGLAS

TABLE OF CONTENTS

TABLE OF CONTENTS

INTRODUCTION

An option is basically an agreement on the underlying shares of stock. It's an agreement to exchange shares at a fixed price over a certain timeframe (they can be bought or sold.) The first thing that you should understand about options is the following. Why would someone get involved with the options trading in the first place? Most people come to options trading with the hope of earning profits from trading the options themselves. And that's probably going to describe most readers of this book. But to truly understand what you're doing, you need to understand why options exist, to begin with.

There are probably three main reasons that options on stocks exist. The first reason is that it allows people that have shares of stock to earn money from their investment in the form of regular income. So, it can be an alternative to dividend income or even enhance dividend income. As we are going to see you later, if you own a minimum of 100 shares of some stock, this is a possibility. Then you can sell options against the stock and earn income from that over time intervals lasting from a week to a month, generally speaking. Obviously, such a move entails some risk, but people will enter positions of that type when the relative risk is low.

The second reason that people get involved with options is that they offer insurance against a collapse of the stock. So, once again, an option involves being able to trade shares on the stock at a fixed price that is set at the time the contract is originated. One type of contract allows the buyer to purchase shares; the other allows the buyer to sell shares. This allows people who own large numbers of shares to purchase something that provides protection of their investment that would allow them to sell the shares at a fixed price, in the event that their stock was declining by huge amounts on the market. So, the concept is exactly like paying insurance premiums. Its unclear how many people actually use this in practice, but this is one of the reasons that options exist. The way this would work would be that you pay someone a premium to secure the right to sell them your stock at a fixed price over some time frame. Then, if the share price drops well below that degree to price, you would still be able to sell your shares and avoid huge losses that were occurring on the market.

The third reason that I would give for the existence of options is that it provides a way for people to make arrangements to purchase shares of stock at the prices that they find attractive, which aren't necessarily available on the market. So, there is a degree of speculation here. But let's just say that a particular stock you are interested in is trading at $100 a share. Furthermore, let's assume that people are extremely bullish on the stock, and they are expecting it to rise by a great deal in the coming weeks. Maybe, it's earnings season.

CHAPTER - 1

OPTION TRADING VARIETY

Available options come in many different types and styles. We will overview some basic expressions that everyone interested in options trading should know and talk in more detail about all of the existing option types.

Firstly, there are Call Options. These options provide you with the right to buy stock labeled as an underlying one. With Call Options, you can buy not only stocks, but also commodities, bonds or any other instrument that has a specified price, otherwise known as the strike price, within a certain timeframe. The Call Options contract gives you the right to buy, but you don't have an obligation to do so. A person who is bullish on the stock is usually the investor who expects the value of the stock to increase shortly. This kind of investor buys call options and manages them in the specified time frame. Again, let's take an example.

Let's say that the investor we will name Mr. B thinks that the next month CCC Company will have bigger earnings for the stock, and the stock will have a higher value. In this case, Mr. B buys a call option for the CCC Company's stock for 20 dollars, for example. The contract of the option has a term that Mr. B can buy up to 100 shares from CCC Company within the next two months. The strike price for these shares within this time frame is 100 dollars. So, if the value of the stock goes below 100 dollars in the next period, Mr. B won't exercise his option, which means that he will lose his original 20 dollars of investment (remember, if the option is not exercised within the specific time frame, or two months in this particular case, the contract expires and becomes worthless.) On the other hand, if the value of the stock goes over 100 dollars, and the next price is 130 dollars, for example, Mr. B can exercise his option. He can now buy the stock for 100 dollars and sell it for 130 dollars on the market. The risk that Mr. B took paid off, and he earned a significant profit.

Secondly, we have Put Options. These options have opposite traits from the Call Options. Put Options represent the contract in which the purchaser has the right to sell his or her stocks. These stocks, like all of the others, have to be sold for the strike price (a price that's been specified for a certain time). Put Options, like

Call Options, give the right to sell, but they are not obligatory. Now we can return to Mr. B and observe him as an investor who is bearish on a certain stock.

In this example, Mr. B thinks that the price of the stock he is interested in will decrease and, in that case, he will purchase a put option. According to Mr. B, the stock that CCC Company has is overpriced, and its value will go lower in the next two months. Let's say that Mr. B buys a Put Option on this stock for 20 dollars again. Contract of the Put Option gives Mr. B a chance to sell the stock he bought from CCC Company for 120 dollars in the next 60 days. So if the stock value increases more than 120 dollars per share, Mr. B won't have to exercise his Put Option, the time frame will pass, and the option will become worthless, which means that he would lose only his initial capital of 20 dollars. However, if the value of the stock goes down, and the price goes from 120 dollars to 90 dollars, for example, the Put Option will be exercised, and Mr. B can sell this stock for 120 dollars per share. Once again, he judged correctly, and he has made a considerable profit.

How to Make a Profit Using Call Options and Put Options

There are many ways for a trader to use Call Options and Put Options and be successful in the process. The best way to show some of the most efficient ways to use these options is by using real numbers. Imagine you want to buy shares from US Bank. Let's suppose that the bank currently sells them for the price of 200 dollars per share and that you conclude that this number is going to go up since the shares are underpriced. Let's also suppose that the predicted amount of time that the shares will need to increase their value is a few months from now. At the moment, you don't have enough capital to buy 100 shares from the US Bank. However, you still want to make some profit from the stock that will rise in value according to your estimation. If this is the case, you can use Call Option and buy it for the stock. This way, you reduce the cost, and you pay only a fraction of the real stock price. Once that you purchased the Call Option, you gained the right to buy 100 shares of US Bank stock for 200 dollars per share in the next two months. One of your doubts might immediately be how are you supposed to buy that stock for 200 dollars per share in the next 60 days when you don't have the initial amount of money for that in the first place? Well, the thing is that you are not under obligation actually to buy the stock if you want to make money. If your estimation is correct and in the next period the value of the stock goes over 200 dollars per share, the Call Option that you bought would increase in value too. In other words, your option contract value rises with the value of the stock price. Keeping this in mind, you get the opportunity to sell your Call Options contract to make money, not the shares. That is the real connection because once when the stock price rises, your contract is worth a lot more than the money you invested to buy it.

A similar thing happens if you purchase the Put Options contract. The only difference is that your estimation has to be decreased in the stock value rather than prices going higher. Once when the underlying security price goes down, the price of your Put Option will go up. The more that the stock price falls, the more expensive your contract becomes. Using options in both cases means that you can make a profit regardless of the rise or fall of the stock prices.

CHAPTER - 2

OPTIONS TRADING STRATEGIES FOR BEGINNERS

The misconception about Options Trading is that it is very difficult to understand, but that is simply not the case. Options are powerful and flexible and can prove to be extremely beneficial if properly used. The way to do that is to gain knowledge about the working and fundamentals of options trading before starting the actual trade.

Covered Call

The covered call strategy generates profits through the means of premiums. There's a term called "Long" for the covered call. This term is used to denote the purchase of assets with the optimism that the value of said assets would rise in the future. Selling call options on this long position enables the investors to generate recurring incomes. Covered calls are neutral in nature, and it is estimated that for the duration of a call option on an asset, the price of the asset will change only minutely, be it high or low. Covered calls are also known as buy-write. Although covered calls provide generous income on short terms, with some patience, it can help the investors to generate income as a chain of premiums. If the investor is willing to wait out, they can choose to keep the underlying assets and not sell them even in the case of a small depression, elevation or inactivity, this works as a protection scheme on long asset position and generate income in premiums. A disadvantage is that if the price of the underlying stock exceeds the price of the option, then the investor has to give up the gains on stocks.

The covered call, being a neutral strategy, means it is not optimal for investors who are very brutish in terms of earning. It is suggested that such investors to keep the stock on hold and not exercise the write option as if the asset price goes up; the option takes the profit on the asset. Also, if the stocks take a big hit, and the estimated loss is going to be too great for recovery from premiums using the call option, the investor should sell the stocks.

Two terms are used for keeping track of profit and loss in this strategy, these are:

The maximum loss—it is calculated by removing the amount received as premium from the purchasing price of the underlying asset.

The maximum profit—it is calculated by calculating the total of the strike price of the short call option and premium received and then subtracting the purchasing price from it.

Married Put

Married put acts as a safety net in the field of options trading. The investor who is holding a long position has to purchase the at-the-money put option to prevent themselves from taking a big hit if the stock prices fall.

The married put is also known as a synthetic long call. Some people may think married put to be similar to covered put, but that is not the case. The married put is optimal for those bullish investors who are wary of probable loss in near-sightedness. Another benefit of implementing the put option is that with this option, the investor gets to enjoy the benefits exclusively available to stockowners such as voting rights and receiving dividends. So is not the case if the investor has invested in a call only option. Same as the covered put, a married put strategy can allow the investors to reap unlimited benefits generated from the initial investment in the underlying stocks. The only deductions from the profit will be the investment used for buying premium of the put option. There's a stage called breakeven at which the price of the underlying asset exceeds the price paid for the options premium. It is after this stage that the profit begins to generate.

Another new term called Floor is used, which is referred to the difference between the actual price at which the underlying stock was purchased, and the strike price of the put. The exercise of a put option falls under the category of married put only when both the assets and the put option are purchased on the same day. The broker is then informed to deliver the bought stocks when the investor exercises their put option.

The question that now arises is, when to use this strategy?

As mentioned in the first line of this concept, married put acts like a safety net or insurance for the investors, and that is how it should be addressed, not as a money-reaping strategy. The price paid for purchasing premium of the put is dedicated to the total profits. This strategy should be used to act as a protection of stocks for short terms so as to counter the probable dip in the stock prices. This gives the investor some sort of reassurance knowing that the chances of loss have been diminished, and they can continue to trade.

Bull Call Spread

Bull Call Spread is ideal for use when a hike in the price of the underlying stock is estimated in the near future by the investor. In Bull Call Spread, the investor has to purchase two specific call options on the same underlying asset and within the month of contract expiration. These two call options are at-the-money call option and out-of-the-money call option. Upon beginning the trade, the Bull Call Spread takes a debit from their account, which is known as the Bull Call Debit Spread.

The cost of implementing bullish options of the trade is eliminated by the sale of out-of-the-money call option.

The total profit is calculated by taking the difference between the strike price of the call options and the bull call debit that was taken at the beginning of the trade. Maximum gain is said to be reached when the price of the underlying assets exceeds the strike prices of the two calls.

Similarly, the maximum loss is calculated by the addition of all the costs incurred in the form of commissions and premiums. An investor faces maximum loss when the prices of the underlying assets fall near to the date of expiration and is either less than or equal to the higher strike price of the two calls.

A few terms are associated with Bull Call Spread which are as follows:

• Break-even point: In the Bull Call Spread, The breakeven point is calculated by the addition of prices of the total premiums purchased and the strike price of the long call.

• Intense Bull Call Spread: Intense Bull Call Spread is determined by subtracting the lower strike price of two call options from the higher one. The investor can reap maximum profits only when the stock prices elevate by a significant margin.

What makes Bull Call Spread alluring to the traders?

There are a number of advantages of the Bull Call Spread strategy that attracts the options traders. These advantages are:

A) There is a certain limit to the loss. Bull Call Spread prevents investors from facing too huge losses.

B) Bull Call Spread generates higher returns from the initial investment than other strategies in which only call options are purchased.

C) More profits are generated when the price of the underlying assets does not rise above the price of the out-of-the-money short call option.

D) Call options can be bought at a lower price

than the strike price.

What are the downsides of Bull Call Spread?

Since Bull Call spread generates more profits than the strategies in which only call options are bought, it means there are more purchases in this strategy than other strategies, which mean cost paid as the commission is higher. Bull Call Spread generates no profits if the price of the underlying asset exceeds the price of the out-of-the-money call option.

What additional steps can you take in Bull Call Spread to strengthen your position?

A) When the prices of the underlying assets are speculated to elevate above the strike price of the short call option, the investor can choose to implement the buy to close option on the out-of-the-money short call and then short it to establish another out-of-the-money call again. Another alternative to that is the investor may just exercise buy to close on the out-of-the-money short call option and leave it at that to reap benefits from the long call option.

B) In a situation where the prices of the underlying assets are not expected to change majorly, the investor can implement an out-of-the-money call option at a higher strike price, this transition the Bull Call spread position to Long Call Ladder spread and the break-even point is decreased.

C) The investor can also transition into Bear Call Spread by closing the long call option. This is ideal for when the price of the underlying stock is speculated to turn back upon reaching the strike price of the short call. The transition has to be done as soon as the price of the underlying stocks becomes equal to the price of a short call.

Bear Put Spread

This strategy is adopted in the situations where a drop in the price of the underlying asset is expected. Bear Put Spread consists of buying put options at a specific strike price and selling an equal number of puts at a lower strike price, which shares the same expiration date.

CHAPTER - 3

BASIC OPTIONS STRATEGIES

If you were first to open your contract by selling, we say that you are "short." If you buy to open a position, we say that you are "long." The simplest way to trade options is to take a long position on a call or a put. Although when buying and selling stocks, we say that someone "shorts" the stock when they are hoping to profit off a decline in share price, you can be hoping to profit from a decline in share price, but you are "long" concerning the put option.

The strategy for profiting from going long on a call or put option is simple. You are hoping the price of the stock would move in your favor so that you will earn a profit. The industry is full of naysayers that downplay this basic strategy; however, the reality is you can earn profits in this way. That is buying or selling individual options, be they the call or put variety. The key to success when doing this type of trading is to stay on top of it and don't buy options on a whim. You need a good reason to buy a call or a put option by itself, and that means paying attention to the financial news surrounding the company, earnings reports, and looking at simple market trends to determine when you have a reasonable probability of earning a profit.

Day Trading and Options

This is just an aside, but watching the movement of a stock price over a single day can provide opportunities to ride a short-term trend in price and profit handsomely. Rising and falling share prices are magnified in the price of the option, so when the share price goes up a few tens of cents, you might profit by $65 or $75 in a single day.

But be aware that the rules for day trading apply to options as well. To be a day trader approved by your broker in the United States, you need to have a margin account, and it needs to have $25,000 deposited in the account. Since options trading often takes place on the level of tens or hundreds of dollars at a time, the vast majority of beginning options traders are not going to be looking to be a day trader. But you are going to be tempted to get out of some trades on the same day that you enter the trade because you might have ridden a trend in one direction or the other to significant profits. The trend might not continue the following day, and you do not want to eat some of your profits from the theta or time decay.

The rule you need to be aware of is if you make four-day trades over five days, which means you will be labeled a pattern day trader. To keep your account open, you'd have to fund it with $25,000. So, this is a situation that you are probably going to want to avoid. To avoid being pulled under by this, simply limit the number of day trades to 3 per week.

Remember that the five-day rule means five consecutive trading days, so weekends do not count. If you made a day trade on Friday, the following Monday, that day, trade still counts against you.

Call Options Basic Strategy

The basic strategy behind making profits with call options is to buy low and sell high. You can profit from this strategy riding a single day's price movement or by "swing trading" the option over one or more days, meaning that you will hold the option overnight. You are not going to hold the option until expiration unless you have the intention of buying the stock.

The time to sell the option is the point at which you have made an acceptable level of profits.

You should set this level beforehand so that you are not letting the emotions of the moment rule your decisions. It's not uncommon to make $50 or $100 profits in a few days or even in a single day off of one option contract, but many traders get dollar signs in their eyes – they get overcome with greed – and as a result, they hold their positions too long. That can mean lost profits, defeat by time decay, or even seeing the option wiped out.

One lesson that you are going to learn is that options prices can fluctuate dramatically. This is because the underlying stock is 100 shares. So a small change in the stock price is magnified by 100 for your investment in the option. Using a one-to-one pricing relationship for the sake of simplicity, if the price of the stock moves up by a mere 45 cents, the price of the option will go up by $45. On the other hand, if it drops by 30 cents, the price of the option would drop $30.

Although the situation of using one-to-one pricing is not realistic, it is pretty clear that small price changes in stock mean significant price changes in your investment.

The key to success with trading options is to have a trading plan that you follow, and which has specific rules.

One skill you are going to need to develop when it comes to calling options is the ability to read stock charts. There are three necessary skills that I recommend you have:

- Learn how to read and interpret candlestick charts.

- Learn how to use moving averages.

- Learn how to use and interpret Bollinger bands.

A candlestick chart divides a stock chart into time intervals that you specify. The time interval you are going to use is going to depend on the time frame over which you are hoping to trade. I have had some success trading call options using a buy to open strategy. I can't say what the situation is in all cases, but what I will tell you is that I don't stay in these trades very long. What I do is I check the early morning financial news for any surprises, and then when the market opens, I look for early indicators of how it is going to move.

If the other aspects of the stock look good – that is, I can buy options with a high level of open interest – then I will enter a position if it looks like there is going to be a strong move over the day or the next few days.

Let's give a few specific examples so that you will have some practical advice for the situation. You can trade index funds like the Dow Jones Industrial Average (trade options on DIA), the S

& P 500 (trade options on SPY), or the NASDAQ (trade options on QQQ). These index funds are susceptible to general economic and political news. So, if you see that a good jobs report has come out, that is a good signal to get in on one or more of these funds. It's often worth the risk to get in on options for these index funds the day before. Then you can wake up and see the results. It's going to be possible to double an investment overnight. Since you are not day trading, in that case, it's a simple matter to exit your positions for a profit. But keep in mind, there is a risk as well if it works against you. If you buy a call, but the early indication is a market sell-off, then get rid of the put first thing when the market opens.

This is an excellent example of why open interest is essential to look at. If you were to buy an option on something with a small level of open interest, you might not be able to get rid of your options before the put lost a lot of money. With something that is very heavily traded like SPY, however, it is a sure bet that you can unload the put quickly.

You also want to pay attention to news about specific companies. For example, if there is news coming out in the early morning hours that the government is going to investigate the social media companies, that is a good indication that going long on a put option would be a reasonable strategy. Conversely, recently, the FTC announced a settlement with Facebook, and this sent the stock soaring.

You are not going to be getting the news "first" as an individual retail investor, but the good news is that with options trading if you are staying on top of things, you are going to be able to get in and out of your trades and take profits if you are careful about it.

Reading the Charts

As an options trader, you are going to have to learn how to read charts. The first thing to do is look up candlestick patterns so that you can recognize when a trend reversal might becoming. Candlestick patterns are not absolute rules or truth-tellers; they are an indicator. So, you consider the candlestick charts and use the entirety of the information that you have available to make your decisions.

As we said earlier, a candlestick can be divided into different timeframes. If you are looking to ride a trend over a single day, a five-minute timeframe is reasonable to use. In this case, each candlestick is going to tell you what the price action was over five minutes.

The candlesticks are going to be colored green or red. If a candlestick is green, it's a "bullish" candlestick. That means that throughout interest, the closing price had risen to a more considerable higher than the opening price. By itself, it does not tell you where the price is headed. For a bullish candlestick, the top of the candle is the price at the end of the trading session, and the bottom of the body is the price at the start.

CHAPTER - 4

VOLATILITY IN THE MARKET

As an options trader, you need to learn about the variables that can affect the price of an option and the ins and outs of implementing the right strategy. A stock trader who is familiar and good with predicting future stock price movement might think that shifting to options trading is easy, but it's not. There are three changing parameters than an options trader must deal with – the underlying stock's price, the time factor, and volatility. A change in any of these factors will affect the price of the option.

The price of an option is also called the premium, and the pricing is per share. The option seller receives the premium which in turn gives the buyer any right that comes along with the option. The buyer is the one paying the premium to the seller, and they can exercise this right or just allow the option to expire without any worth in the end. The buyer is obliged to pay the premium whether the option is exercised or not, which means the seller will keep the premium, in the end, no matter what.

Let's have a simple example. A buyer paid a seller for purchasing rights to stock ABC for 100 shares and a strike price at $60. The contract expires on June 19. If the option position becomes profitable, the option will be exercised by the buyer. If it does not seem to bear profit, the buyer can just let the contract expire. The seller then keeps the premium.

There are two sides to the premium of an option – its intrinsic and time value. You can compute for an option's intrinsic value by getting the difference between the strike price and the stock price. For the call option, it is the stock price minus the strike price. For the put option, it is the strike price minus the stock price.

To value an option, at least theoretically, you will need to consider multiple variables such as the underlying stock price, volatility, exercise price, time to expiration, and interest rate. These factors will provide you a good estimate on the fair value of an option that you can then incorporate into your strategy for maximum gains.

The value of puts and calls are affected by underlying stock price movements straightforwardly. That means when the price of a stock rises, there should be a corresponding rise in call value as well since you can purchase the underlying stock at a reduced price compared to the market's, while there is price decrease in put. Conversely, there should be an increase in the value of put options when the price of the stock takes a dive and a decrease in the value of call options since the holder of the put option has the option to sell the stock at above-market prices. This pre-set price at which you can sell or buy is called the strike price of the option or its exercise price. If the option's strike price gives you the advantage of selling or buying the stock at a cost that gives you immediate profit, that option is considered 'in the money.'

Time

Time is money. This adage still holds true and even applies to options trading. Thus, understanding how the Greek theta works is very important and how it affects the pricing of options. If you still remember, the Greek letter theta represents the effect of time decay on the value of an option. All options, call or put, lose their value as the contract expiration nears, but the value loss rate of an option contract is a function of the amount of time remaining before it expires.

The extrinsic part of the value of an option is the only factor affected by time decay. That means an option that's 'in the money' will have the same intrinsic value until the contract expires. For example, if a stock trades at $3, a call for a 30-strike price will retain its intrinsic value of $3 from the start until expiration, but any value that exceeds $3 is considered extrinsic value and will be affected by the time decay.

However, theta does change over time. Let's assume that a stock's price remains unchanged, a $2.75 'out of the money' option with a -0.15 theta will have a reduced value of $2.60 by the following day. The theta then may only be set to -0.12, which means the cost of the option will be down to $2.48 the succeeding day if stock prices remain unchanged. The option's value will gradually approach zero while it's still 'out of the money.'

You also need to remember that the effect of theta becomes more and more apparent as the expiration nears. You should anticipate a rapid acceleration of the time decay within the remaining few days before the contract expires.

Options that are 'at the money' possess the highest value, extrinsically. That's why these options have their thetas set to highest. Options that are deep 'in the money' or 'out of the money' have their thetas lower because compared to 'at the money options,' they have lower extrinsic values. And the less extrinsic value an option has, the less they will lose as time decays.

The only way for the theta position to be positive is to have short options. This is because short option positions work best when the market is stable. Wide swings both up or down hurt option positions and only time will help as it passes by. Other strategies, also benefit from time's passage, such as neutral strategies, e.g., long butterfly. The less time there is before the contract expires, the less probability for the underlying stock to rise up or go down and reach unprofitable territories.

There will always be a trade-off between market movement and time for every option position. It's impossible to benefit from the two at the same time. If time is helping your option position, it will be negatively affected by the price movement.

Volatility

Volatility affects most investment forms to some degree, and as an option trader, you should be familiar with this element and how it affects options pricing. By definition, volatility is the tendency of something to fluctuate or change significantly. In general investment, volatility refers to the rate a financial instrument price rises or falls.

A low volatility financial instrument has a price that is relatively stable. Conversely, a high volatility financial instrument is prone to dramatic price changes, either way. In general, financial market volatility can be broadly measured. So when the market becomes difficult to predict, and prices keep on regularly and rapidly changing, the market is volatile

Volatility can affect option pricing significantly. Many beginning options traders tend to ignore the implications which can lead to huge investment losses.

Historical Volatility

Historical or statistical volatility is used to measure the changes in the price of the underlying option, so it's based on actual and real data. Let's refer to it as HV for the rest. HV shows how fast the stock price has moved. The higher HV is, the more the stock price has moved during a certain period. So when a stock has a high HV, the price is more likely to move, at least theoretically. It's more of a future movement indication and not a real guarantee.

On the other hand, a low HV might indicate the stock price hasn't moved much, but it might be going in one direction steadily.

You can use HV to predict somewhat how much a security's price will change based on how fast it changed in the past, but you can't use it to predict an actual trend.

HV is measured over a certain period, such as a week, month, or year and you can compute for it in various ways.

Implied Volatility

Another type of volatility that options traders should be aware of if implied volatility or IV. Whereas HV measures a security's past volatility, IV is more of an estimate of its future volatility.

IV is a projection of how fast and how much the stock price is likely to change in price. Many beginning traders focus on the profitability (difference in strike price and stock price) and the contract expiration when considering an option's price, but IV also plays a major role.

You can determine an option's IV by considering factors such as the stock and strike prices, length of time before expiration, current interest rate, and HV. Since an option's IV may indicate how much the stock will change in price, the price gets higher when the IV itself increases. Because theoretically, more profit can be gained when there are dramatic movements in the price of the underlying stock. The price of an option can also change significantly even when the price of the stock itself remains the same, and this is usually caused by its IV.

For example, ABC is about to release a new product, and speculations are building up that the company is about to announce it. The options' IV for stock ABC can be very high since there are expectations of significant movement in the price of the underlying stock. The announcement might be received well, and the price of the stock might go up, or the audience will be disappointed with the new product, and stock prices can drop quickly. In this scenario, the price of the stock might not move significantly since investors will be waiting for the press release before buying or selling stocks. There will then be increased in extrinsic value for both puts and calls, rather than movement in the stock price. This is one way that IV can affect option pricing.

If you're betting that a stock's price will dramatically increase once that announcement has been made, you may purchase 'at the money' call options to maximize probable gains for that increase. If after ABC made the announcement and was received well, causing the stock prices to shoot up, then there would have been significant gains in the call options' intrinsic value. After the press release and the stock price movement, IV will then be lower since it's predicted that the stock price won't change so much very soon. There will then be a substantial fall on the calls' extrinsic value, and that would offset most of the profit you gained with the increased intrinsic value.

CHAPTER - 5

BEGINNERS COMMON MISTAKES

Trading options are more involved than trading stocks, so there are ample opportunities to make mistakes. It's important to take the approach of going small and slow at first so that you don't lose the shirt off your back. That said, if you run into mistakes, don't get too down about it. Dust yourself off and get up to fight another day. With that said, let's have a look at some common mistakes and how to avoid them.

Putting All Your Eggs in One Basket

While there is a difference between investing and trading, traders can learn a few things from our investor brothers (and most people are a little of both anyway). Don't let everything ride on one trade. If you take all the money you have and invest it in buying options for one stock, you're making a big mistake. Doing that is very risky, and as a beginning trader, you're going to want to mitigate your risk as much as possible. Betting on one stock may pay off sometimes, but more times than not it's going to lead you into bankruptcy territory.

Investing More than You Can

It's easy to get excited about options trading. The chances to make fast money and the requirements that you analyze the markets can be very enticing. Oftentimes that leads people into getting more excited than they should. A good rule to follow with investing is to make sure that you're setting aside enough money to cover living expenses every month, with a security fund for emergencies. Don't bet the farm on some sure thing by convincing yourself that you'll be able to make back twice as much money and so cover your expenses. Things don't always work out.

Going All in Before You're Ready

Another mistake is failing to take the time to learn options trading in real time. Just like getting overly excited can cause people to bet too much money or put all their money on one stock, some people are impatient and don't want to take the time to learn the options markets by selling covered calls. It's best to start with covered calls and then move slowly to small deals buying call options. Leave put options until you've gained some experience.

Failure to Study the Markets

Remember, you need to be truly educated to make good options trades. That means you'll need to know a lot about the companies that you're either trying to profit from or that you're shorting. Options trading isn't possible without some level of guesswork, but make your guesses, educated guesses, and don't rely too much on hunches.

Not Getting Enough Time Value

Oftentimes, whether you're trading puts or calls, the time value is important. A stock may need an adequate window of time in order to beat the stock price, whether it's going above it or plunging below it. When you're starting out and don't know the markets as well as a seasoned trader, you should stick to options you can buy that have a longer time period before expiring.

Not Having Adequate Liquidity

Sometimes beginning investors overestimate their ability to play the options markets. Remember that if you buy an option, to make it work for you—you're going to need money on hand to buy stocks when the iron is hot. And you're going to need to buy 100 shares for every option contract. Before entering into the contract, make sure that you're going to be able to exercise your option.

Not Having a Grip on Volatility

If you don't understand volatility and its relation to premium pricing, you may end up making bad trades.

Failing to Have a Plan

Trading seems exciting, and when you're trading, you may lose the investors' mentality. However, traders need to have a strategic plan as much as investors do. Before trading, make sure that you have everything in place, including knowing what your goals are for the trades, having pre-planned exit strategies, developing criteria for getting into a trade so that you're not doing on a whim or based on emotion.

Ignoring Expiration Dates

It sounds crazy, but many beginners don't keep track of the expiration date. Would you hate to see a stock go up in price, and then hope it keeps going up, and it does, only to find out that your expiration date passed before you exercised your option?

Overleveraging

It's easy to spend huge amounts of money in small increments. This is true when it comes to trading options. Since stocks are more expensive, it's possible to get seduced by purchasing low priced options. After all, options are available at a fraction of the cost that is required to buy stocks. And you might keep on purchasing them until you're overleveraged.

Buying Cheap Options

In many cases, buying cheap things, isn't a good strategy. If you're buying a used car, while you might occasionally find a great car that is a good buy, in most cases, a car is cheap for a reason. The same applies to options trading. When it comes to options, a cheap premium probably denotes the option is out of the money. Sure, you save some money on a cheap premium, but when the expiration date comes, you might see the real reason the option contract was a cheap buy. Of course, as we described earlier, there may be cases where cheaper options have the capacity to rebound and become profitable by the time the expiry date arrives. But taking chances like that is best left to experienced traders.

Giving in to Panic

Remember that you have the right to buy or sell a stock if you've purchased an option. Some beginners panic and exercise their right far too early. This can happen because of fears that they'll be missing out an opportunity with a call option, or because of fears that a stock won't keep going down on a put.

Not Knowing How Much Cash You Can Afford to Lose

Going into options trading blindly is not a smart move. With each option trade you make, you need to have a clear idea of how much cash you have on hand to cover losses and exercising your options. You'll also want to know how much cash you can afford to lose if things go south.

Jumping into Puts Without Enough Experience and Cash to Cover Losses

Remember, if you're selling puts, you will have to buy the stock at the strike price if the buyer exercises their option. This is a huge risk. The stock could have plunged in value, and you're going to have to buy the stock at the strike price, possibly leaving you with huge losses. Don't go into selling puts with your eyes closed, in fact, beginners are better off avoiding selling puts. But if you must do it, make sure you can absorb the losses when you bet wrong.

Piling It On

Most beginner mistakes are related to panic. If you're looking at losses on options, some beginners double and triple up, hoping to make it up when things turn better. Instead, they end up losing more money. Instead of giving in to panic, learn when to cut your losses and re-evaluate your trading strategy.

Staying in a Written Contract When You Should Get Out

If you've sold an option and it's looking like you might face a loss, you can always get out of it by selling.

CHAPTER - 6

PITFALLS TO AVOID

You will encounter downturns from time to time, especially during trading. If not dealt with, you may end up burnt out and extremely frustrated. You must know how to handle yourself in these cases to avoid further despair. For making the best out of a bad situation, the following pointers may be of help to you:

- Embrace your failure and accept it

- Do not avoid addressing your shortcomings, however embarrassing they may be

- Take personal responsibility and avoid blaming others

- Analyze your actions and identify where you went wrong

- Consider whether you would have handled the situation differently

- Listen to the opinions and advice of your colleagues

- Learn from the situation and rectify your relevant behavioral aspect

- Avoid repeating the error or mistake in a similar situation in the future

The Misconceptions and Pitfalls of Options Trading

A long call option is useful when you expect a stock price to rise in the future. You engage in long call options whenever you feel very bullish about a particular stock. This strategy is aggressive and relies on your confidence in rising future stock prices. Your potential for profits is unlimited since the expected upward trend maintains the trajectory assuming all factors remain the same. However, your risk is limited to the premium since you make losses when the stock price remains or falls below the strike price.

A short call option is strategically opposite to a long call option. In this case, you are hoping and predicting that stock prices will fall in the future. You have to be particularly bearish to engage in short call options. If the stock price follows your predicted downward trend, you make a profit. Short calls are risky since your profit margin is limited to the premium while your risk exposure is unlimited. You may end up with substantial losses should the stock prices reverse direction and start rising in value.

Tips You Can Apply to Succeed in Options Trading

You need abundant knowledge and experience to trade in options successfully. However, since it will take time for you to gain the relevant experience, you may apply the following tips during trading:

Evaluate your choices

Evaluating your choices before delving into options trading is akin to conducting due diligence. You want to have all pertinent information available to you before investing in options. Such due diligence will put you on a path to eventual profitability in the end.

Failure in conducting this evaluation might lead you to unimaginable losses due to unforeseen pitfalls associated with options trading. Trading in options primarily involves buying and selling of options. You need to have a grasp of all the available options from which to choose. Having a keen eye for profitability will serve you well in the long run. You will soon realize that trading options is quite different from outright buying and selling a stock. You should never confuse these two different investment strategies.

A proper evaluation of available investment strategies will clear this confusion for you. You should first have the knowledge related to options trading and understand all the terminologies involved. You need not just identify the lingo, but learn the meaning of every term in options trading. You will be wise to consult an experienced professional or brokerage firm to get a full understanding of both the advantages and downsides of trading options.

Set your objectives

What do you aim to achieve from trading options? You must clearly state and write down your goal at the beginning of options trading. Your stated purpose should be specific, time-bound, measurable, and transparent. Do not set out with abstract goals that do not have any specificity. Such poor objectives include statements like I want to make a lot of money at the end of my options trade.

This goal is not specific enough. A better explanation of objective should sound something like; I will make a profit of X dollars within a Y time frame. Your goal is then specific to the amount of money you will be aiming to make and is time-bound within a specified period. In addition to having a set-out objective, you must develop your investment policy statement. This policy will provide you with strict guidelines to follow during your trading. It protects you from deviating from the laid down course of actions.

Besides, your policy statement needs to identify the potential pitfalls that may hamper your path towards success and provide ways of tackling the challenges. You need to promptly devise a way to either avoid or address such challenges according to your policy guidelines. Every investment strategy faces risks, and options trading will be no different. You must assess your risks against your objectives and adjust accordingly. Once you have a clear goal, then your decision-making should be focused on achieving your overall objective by the end of your set expiry period.

Identify profitable options

Your main aim for investing in options is to make profits. Therefore, you need to have an eye or a killer instinct for identifying opportunities that have a high potential for returns. Options trading deal with the potential future stock price movements in a particular direction. You need to be able to predict the next price trend of a given stock correctly based on current factors available to you. It is a test of your speculative ability.

Your ability to identify this trend typically

develops with experience. The more you trade-in options, the more your knack to define valuable options will improve. Remember, your options become profitable only if the stock trend follows your earlier prediction. This prediction is also time-bound; hence, your forecast has to come true within a specific period. In direct stock trading, you make profits from increased stock value over time. An options trade makes money from a correct trajectory of the stock price over the same period.

You could predict a downward trend and make a profit if the stock price correspondingly trends downwards over the specified period. However, in a direct stock trade, a downward trend would indicate a loss of value in your particular stock. To increase your chances of identifying profitable options, you need a keen eye for the market trends and any associated factors affecting volatility. Stock volatility is directly related to options profitability. Such a stock guarantees you future price movements, and the only unknown is the kind of trajectory.

Conduct intelligent trades

Now that you have identified your potentially profitable options, it is time to make your entry into the options market. During trading, follow this straightforward rule: You should always make a habit of buying options contracts that are underpriced while selling the overpriced contracts. Also, you should know when to make your move rather than the number of steps you make. Your timing is more valuable than the quantity.

This way, you end up gaining overall value from your particular option. The historical volatility of a given stock will influence your predictability of the future price movements of that particular stock. Therefore, having available data on this volatility is vital for the profitability potential of your trades. You should not spend a lot of time feeling the market and trying to make your decisions based on your market emotions. When you do this, you will certainly lose your investment. Also, wasting time in overanalyzing the minor underlying factors affecting stock prices will take too much of your time.

Remember, your options contract is time-bound, and it depreciates, the closer you approach to your expiry date. Intelligent trading is a well-informed piece of business when it comes to trading options. Here are some examples of call and put options that explain the value of smart trading. When you deal with call options, you should buy your option contract at a lower strike price than your projected future value of the associated stock.

When the worth of the stock goes up as you

intended, the value of your option also rises. Your option contract is in the money and, most importantly, is profitable. Once the stock price has gained the maximum amount it possibly can during the period, your best move is to sell your call option. This way, you will have made a significant profit since the only way the stock can move from here onwards is to trend downwards.

When you keep waiting for a more extended gain momentum, your option starts losing value since the stock price starts falling. In this case, you either let the option expire and make a loss or exercise its time value and gain some benefit, albeit a small amount. This option roll out would be preferable from your depreciating option.

On the other hand, you own a put option that you are considering selling. First, you need to buy put options at a much higher strike price than your projected future minimum stock value. Since you expect the stock price to fall over the particular period, your put option remains profitable during this duration. Your intelligent move would be to exercise the option at the minimum stock value.

After the downward trend, the only way the stock can go from here is a trend upwards. When you sell your put option at the stock's minimum value point, then you will have made a significant profit from that trade. However, if you delay exercising your option contract, your contract's value will start falling since the stock price will be trending upwards. Just like the call option, a put option depreciates as you approach its expiry date. In this case, you may avoid a total loss by exercising the option's time value instead of letting it expire.

CHAPTER - 7

HOW OPTIONS PRICES ARE DETERMINED

Right before you start venturing into the world of options trading, as an investor, you need to have a proper understanding of the several factors that determine the value of options. The factors include the intrinsic value, the current price of the stock, expiration time, rates of interest, volatility, and paid cash dividends. You might come across various models of options pricing that uses up all of these parameters for determining the option fair value of the market. In several ways, options trading is more or less like any other branch of investment, all that you need is to understand all those factors that are used for pricing them.

For starting, let's begin with the most important drivers of options price: the current price of the stock, intrinsic value, volatility, and expiration time. The current price of the stock is somewhat very obvious. The movement of the stock price up or down comes with a direct, but not equal, effect on the option price. When the price of the stock rises, the price of a call option is most likely to rise as well, and the price of the put option will fall down. When the price of the stock tends to fall, the reverse takes place for the prices of puts and calls.

Intrinsic value

It is the value that any option would have if the option is exercised today. In simple terms, intrinsic value is the overall amount by which option strike price is within the money. It is also that portion of the price of an option that is no lost when time seems to exceed the expiration time or when it is near the expiration time. Calculation of the intrinsic value of any call or put option is quite easy and can be done in this way:

Intrinsic value of call option = USC – CS, in which USC stands for underlying stock's current price, and CS stands for call strike price.

The option intrinsic value can directly reflect the effective nature of financial advantage that can result if the concerned option is exercised immediately. In simple terms, it can also be regarded as the minimum value of an option. Options trading out of the money or at the money do not come with any form of intrinsic value.

Intrinsic value of put option = PS – USC, in which PS stands for put strike price, and USC stands for underlying stock's current price.

For instance, say the stock of Elegant Electric (EE) is selling out at $35. The EE 20 call option would have the intrinsic value of $15 ($35-$20 = $15) as the holder of the option can easily exercise the option for buying shares of EE at $20, turn around, and then automatically sell them out in the market for $35 and have a profit of $15.

Time value

The time value, often known as the extrinsic value, is the total amount by which the option price exceeds the option intrinsic value. It is directly linked to the total amount of time that any option has in hand until the date of expiry.

The formula for the time value of options is quite easy:

Time value = Price of option – Intrinsic value

The more time that any option has in its hand until the date of expiry, the more are the chances of it ending up in the money. The component of time of any option tends to decay exponentially. The actual derivative of the option time value is actually a complex equation. As the general rule, an option will be losing its one-third value right during the first half of the life of the option and will lose two-thirds in the second half. This is a very important aspect for the security investors as the closer is the expiration time, the more movement will be needed at the price of the underlying assets for impacting the option price.

The time value of an option is also dependent on market volatility. For the stocks that are not expected to have much movement, the time value of the option will tend to be very low. For all those stocks that are not expected to have much movement, the time value of the option will tend to be low. The opposite is also true for the more volatile stocks.

Volatility

The overall effect of volatility is, most of the time, difficult and subjective for quantifying.

There are various types of calculators available today for calculating the estimated volatility. There are several types of volatility that you are most likely to come across while dealing with options trading. HV or historical volatility helps in determining the most possible magnitude of the future moves of any underlying stocks. Two-thirds of all possible occurrences of the price of a stock will take place within minus or plus of the stock's one single standard deviation move over a fixed period of time. HV is used for showing the volatile nature of any market.

Implied volatility is implied by using the current prices of the market and is often used up with the theoretical models. It helps a lot in setting up the current price of any existing option. It also helps the players of options to assess the trade potential properly. Implied volatility is used for measuring the expected upcoming volatility for an options trader. In simple terms, it can indicate the present sentiment of the options market. This very sentiment will then be reflected directly in the options price and thus helping the traders in assessing the future option volatility and also of the stock-based only on the current prices of the option.

Any investor of stocks who is really interested in using up options for capturing the potential nature of move in a particular stock needs to understand the overall process of how options are being priced. Having proper knowledge of the current and also the expected volatility in the options price is also essential for any type of investor who is willing to take full advantage of the stock price movement, up or down.

CHAPTER - 8

FINANCIAL LEVERAGE

The process of using borrowed capital (debt) to increase the shareholder's return on their investments or equity in capital structure is called financial leverage or Trading on equity. The financial leverage analyzed by the firm is intended to earn more return on the fixed charge funds rather than their costs. The surplus will increase the return on the owner's equity, whereas the deficit will decrease the return on the owner's equity. Financial leverage affects the EPS (Earnings per share). When the EBIT increases, then EPS increases.

For example, if the firm borrows a debt from creditors for $1000 at 7% interest per annum, i.e., $70 and invests this debt to earn a 12% return on this, i.e., $120 per annum. Then the difference of surplus, i.e., $50, which is after interest payment made to the creditors of the firm, will belong to the shareholders or owners of the firm, and it is referred to as profit from financial leverage. Conversely, if the firm would earn a 5% return, then the firm has a loss of $20 (i.e., $70 - $50) to the shareholders.

Highly leveraged companies may be at risk of bankruptcy if they are unable to make a payment on their debt, but it can increase shareholder's return on their investment, and there are tax advantages associated with leverage.

Financial leverage ratio = EBIT / EBT

The financial leverage ratio is used to analyses the Capital structure and financial risk of the company. It explains how the fixed interest-bearing loan capital affects the operating profit of the firm. If EBIT is more than EBT, this ratio becomes more than 1. A slightly higher ratio is favorable, i.e., if this ratio is marginally more than 1 that is nearer to 1, it indicates moderate use of debt capital, low financial risk, and good financial judgment.

Why Is Leverage Riskier?

Another significant risk to be aware of is that of leverage. Because Options don't cost much as stock as they are simply a contract, this means that they experience disproportionately larger percentage price gains in reaction to the far more expensive underlying stock's very small price movements. The huge benefit of this is that it results in large percentage gains when the underlying stock moves in the anticipated direction by even a small amount. The downside, though, is that it also results in a 100% wipe-out of the investment if the stock moves by even the smallest amount in the wrong direction. This is not necessarily an issue with beginners, or at least it shouldn't be as the risk manifests itself mainly through trading too large a position size. However, you need to be aware that as beneficial as leverage is, it can also be a double-edged sword, so be aware that leverage is a risk that needs to be addressed. One simple way to nullify or minimize this level of risk is to keep your position size small.

Lastly, Options, as we know, possesses a time value (extrinsic value) in addition to their inherent intrinsic value (in the money value), which is also another double-edged sword. For option buyers, time-decay acts as a headwind because it is continually decreasing the value of the option. By doing so, this increases the dependency on greater stock price movement to break even on the trade. For option writers, it acts as a tailwind because it allows a profit to be generated through steady premium incomes regardless of whether the stock moves or not.

The Advantages of Leverage in Options Trading

The options exchanges play a critical role in ensuring that there are enough securities to base options contracts on. Following are some of the significant functions of an options exchange.

Liquidity

Perhaps the biggest function of options exchanges is to ensure ready markets for options contracts. The markets ensure that holders of options can exercise their options and that there are enough buyers to purchase the options. Traders are looking for avenues to increase their earning potential, and liquidity helps them achieve that. Options contracts have a time limit, unlike other securities such as shares, which necessitates liquidity. The existence of market makers is particularly responsible for liquidity.

Gauging a country's economy

The state of an options market can reliably inform us what the country's economic situation is like. The most common underlying assets that traders base their options on our shares. The prevailing economic conditions are always reflected in the share prices of various companies. If the country is experiencing prosperity, the share prices will be up, and if the country is experiencing market crashes, the share prices will go down. Thus, the options exchanges play a critical role in ensuring that traders have a sense of how their country is performing economy-wise. Stocks are the pulse of an economy, and they are accurate predictors of a country's economic state.

Securities pricing

Options traders have a wide pool to choose from when it comes to underlying assets. However, the value of an underlying asset is determined by the options exchange according to the forces of demand and supply. The financial securities of prosperous companies are worth more than the securities of moderately successful companies. The valuation of securities is important not only for traders but also for governments. Governments levy taxes on earnings drawn from options trading, so they first have to get the value of the securities.

Safety of transactions

Traders want to be sure that they can trust all the parties that they are getting into business with. Therefore, it is the work of an options exchange to ensure the players are trustworthy. For one, most options contracts are based on financial securities of publicly listed companies, and these companies must operate within stringent rules and regulations. Thus, the trader is assured of security when dealing with other parties. The options markets should provide all relevant information about options contracts and securities to discourage the trader from making a move out of ignorance.

Providing speculation scope

Speculation of securities is critical to ensure a healthy balance of demand and supply of securities. Many traders earn their profits from purely speculative risk. They have developed a skill of determining the movement of prices. The options exchanges provide traders with the resources and tools of speculating on the securities performance, thus allowing traders to earn profits.

Promotes an investment culture

Options exchanges are critical in promoting the culture of investing in valuable securities like the stock as opposed to unproductive assets such as precious metals. Traders have a wide selection of underlying securities to base their options contracts on; thus, they are not limited in the range of their strategies. A strong saving and investment culture is critical for the economic advancement of a country.

The continuous market for securities

Options exchanges allow traders to base their options on a wide range of underlying securities, and in case of any risks, traders are at liberty to switch from one security to the subsequent. This is different from purchasing stocks wherein you are stuck with the consequences of poor decisions.

Capital formation

Options exchanges promote the pooling together and redistribution of resources. The exchanges create a win-win situation for both sides. Companies raise capital when their stocks are publicly listed, and their securities act as the underlying. On the other hand, traders stand to benefit from the high earning potential and low-capital requirements for options contracts. So, options exchanges play a critical role in ensuring that the parties are in a position to generate capital.

Control companies

The significance of transparency within the derivatives market cannot be overstated. If a trader has the misfortune of working with shady companies, they could easily lose their earnings. Options exchanges make it hard for shady companies to spoil the market. For instance, publicly traded companies have to submit relevant documents and adhere to certain performance standards, as doing so will boost investor confidence. Companies that refuse to cooperate with exchanges are blacklisted from the market.

Fiscal and monetary policies

The fiscal policy and the monetary policy of the government must not hurt the players in the financial industry. Options exchanges facilitate the creation and execution of key policies that will govern the financial markets.

Proper canalization of wealth

Options are a great way of putting capital into greater use, as opposed to having the capital just sitting around. Thus, the economy benefits from an injection of capital, which would otherwise have been inactive. The injection of capital into the economy promotes wealth distribution and fights off economic disgraces like unemployment.

Education purposes

Options trading features complex processes. Even people who claim to understand options trading might be low-key deluded. Thus, the importance of education cannot be overstated. Many traders just get the hang of things and set about purchasing and selling options contracts, forgetting that it is critical first to educate one's self. Options exchanges provide a wealth of resources and information that are meant to enlighten traders. Empowered traders improve trading activity.

Disadvantages of Leverage in Options Trading

Again, I won't bore you with elaborate explanations of the disadvantages of options trading. Instead, here's another helpful list that clearly outlines why traders might choose to shy away from potential options trading opportunities:

- Options are time-sensitive investments. Yes, you can pick and choose options based on expiration dates, but you'll always be confined to a certain expiration date where you must choose to act or choose to exit.

- Successful options trading requires your attention and time. Without it, you risk losing out on potential profit-generating opportunities that come from buying or selling your call or put option at the right, most profitable time.

- Options are without a paper-trail. With stocks and bonds, for example, you'll receive some sort of paper certification regarding your investment. Options are "book-entry" investments, meaning you receive no paper certification that shows your claim to an option or your ownership of an option.

- You're working in the stock market, a highly volatile place where changes occur suddenly and dramatically. You'll need to be on constant alert, or at least hire a broker who will.

- You'll need to be in a somewhat stable financial situation before you can successfully trade. Establishing and frequently adding to some sort of "trading fund" before you begin your options, trading endeavors will somewhat remedy an unstable financial situation, however.

CHAPTER - 9

STOCK PICKING

Stay Away from Penny Stocks

Beginners must stay away from penny stocks. Penny stocks can be treacherous and deceptive for new traders. I have nothing against penny stocks. Many people like to trade in penny stocks as they are cheap, and they can give great momentum. These two qualities that make them a darling of most small budget traders. However, these are the very qualities due to which every trader must stay away from penny stocks. It's very hard to tell which way the stock would move, and most of the companies that penny stocks trading in are shady.

As a beginner, your focus should remain to trade in solid stocks that have a proven track record of performance. Therefore, whosoever may push them to you, stay away from the penny stocks.

Qualities to Look For

Liquidity

Many things in the market can make the life of a trader difficult, and poor liquidity would easily top the list among them. Liquidity in the stocks means the volume or the number of shares getting traded in a day. If a stock has poor liquidity, then selling the stocks or squaring off your position in that stock would become difficult.

Stocks with poor liquidity are also easy to manipulate. Even a limited number of big traders can create fake momentum in such stocks, and you might fall into that trap.

Another big issue with low liquidity stocks is a wider spread. The difference between the bid price and the asking price is so high that most traders are not able to close their positions profitably.

In the beginning, you must only choose stocks with good liquidity.

Mind the Volatility

Volatility in the stock market isn't a bad thing. A certain level of volatility is desirable in good stocks so that you can make money trading them in a round-trip within one session.

However, if the whole market is highly volatile, or a certain stock has become very volatile due to certain news, result declaration, litigation, or any other positive or negative information, you must avoid trading in such a stock. Certain strategies can help you in making money through options trade, but when a stock is highly volatile, trading can be really risky.

Most of the action in a highly volatile stock is within a few minutes, and by the time most day traders enter into that stock, it starts to move in the opposite direction. Therefore, it is better to avoid such mayhem and let the market settle down a bit before you place your trade. As a beginner, your focus must remain on making normal trades in a normal market.

Good Correlation Stocks

Although the stock market runs on uncertainty, yet every trader likes to lean on dependable stocks. Stocks that don't perform erratically always have a better scope for a day trader, as mapping them becomes easier. These are called Correlative Stocks because they have a very strong correlation with the movement of specific sectors, indices, and segments.

As a new trader, your focus should also be on such stocks that are not very unpredictable. You may not see very sudden or erratic moves in them, but that would also save you from several unpleasant surprises.

Stocks That Follow the Market Trend

We have always been taught to be different and swim against the tide. We have been told that the winners don't follow the league create one of their own. Well, when it comes to the stock market, you wouldn't want to bet on such winners to start with.

Such stocks can give you an excellent start, but there is no way in the world that you will be able to predict them. They are rocky and risky.

It is always better to find the stocks which follow the market trend. This simply means that look for those stocks that run as the market runs. If the markets are bullish, these stocks will rise with the market. If the market sentiment is bearish, they will show a negative trend. Such stocks will give you a chance to earn money both in the bull runs as well as bear runs.

Most of the stable stocks show such movements. You can rely on them, and taking a position and getting out of it on the same day in such stocks is comparatively easy. You wouldn't want to get into a stock that's rising when the market is falling, and as soon as you put your money in it, the movement stops or takes an opposite turn. Such stocks are very dangerous, and there are plenty of them out there. Sticking with the big and reliable ones can help you in preventing such issues.

Good Fundamentals

Although many experts would say that fundamental analysis doesn't play an important role in day trading, don't get sold on that completely. When the mood of the market is bad, only these kinds of stocks survive. The reason is simple when the tide is over, and the traders like to go with safer options.

Stocks with good fundamentals will always be more reliable and dependable. The market trusts them. Even small news about their profits and expansion can bring big moves in such stocks. You may not find such movement in smaller stocks even with big news because most traders don't trust them.

Initially, only trade with stocks that have good fundamentals. They will help you understand the way market functions, and once you feel you are ready, you can also start trying others.

Ownership Pattern

This is another very important point that usually gets ignored. Stocks are held by retail investors and traders like me and you and also by institutional investors. Both types of investors have different buying and selling patterns.

A retail investor can dump all the held shares with the drop of a hat. As soon as a piece of bad news comes, the retail investors are the first to exit. However, institutional investors can't do that. They maintain very large portfolios, and their decision-makers need to have approval at several levels. This means a stock in which institutional investors also have a good stake will be more reliable as they'll have a lot of volatility even after a major news event. The slow response of the institutional investors also ensures that there is no panic or crisis like situation all of a sudden because a lot of stocks are locked with them.

Looking at the ownership pattern of stocks can help you in understanding the risk involved with the stock. If a stock is primarily held by retail investors, there can be no definite knowledge about the people who hold them. It can be just a group of certain individuals who can start creating momentum in the stock artificially. They can also dump all the shares all of a sudden. Institutional investors simply can't do that.

As a new trader, trade in the stocks in which institutional investors like mutual funds, hedge funds, etc. have a good stake. Such trading will keep your risk contained.

Understandable Chart Patterns

Once you start reading the technical charts, you'll find that some stocks make real sense on the charts. They follow patterns. Their movements are somewhat predictable. They aren't very jumpy or choppy. While doing this, you'll also come across stocks that don't follow any pattern. They don't correlate to the indices or segments. They are vagabonds. Such stocks are risky for day trading.

One thing that every day trader must engrave on to their minds is you don't want to get stuck with a stock forever. No matter how good or bad that stock is. You want a quick in and out of that stock. The stocks that don't follow an understandable pattern can get stuck with you. Once you buy them, understanding or predicting their movement will become difficult, and you won't find a way out.

The best way out is to look for stocks that have an understandable chart pattern. The stocks that are moving in a definite pattern are always a better bet.

Sensibility to the New Flow

Last but not least, sensibility to the news flow can be a big asset for an intraday stock. Some stocks react great to news events and give a good trading opportunity. However, some stocks would remain dormant, no matter what kind of news pours in. They are thick-skinned and become unpredictable as far as trading is concerned. You should avoid such stocks.

Look for stocks that show a great movement and sensibility to news events and give you trading opportunities.

High Volume

No matter how good the stock looks, if it does not have the volume, it is not fit for intraday trading. Don't fall for such stocks as the risk of getting caught in them will be very high. This is the first and foremost quality you must look for while picking your stock of the day for trading.

Testing Support and Resistance Levels

Look for stocks that are testing their support or resistance levels. These stocks can give a breakout, and you will have a great opportunity to earn from such stocks. Examine their levels carefully and study their historical patterns. If they have done that even in the past, it can be a great sign.

Near 52 Weeks Low or High

Stocks that are near their 52 weeks low or high can also give you a good opportunity to trade. Such traders can make a breakout and set new targets, and hence if you can correlate that with the fundamentals of these stocks, you can build an opportunity to trade.

Gainers or Losers of the Week

These stocks will be in the news and, therefore, trading in these stocks can be a good idea. However, you'll have to remain cautious as a stock that has been continuously gaining for some time can't continue to do so. You'll have to study whether the stock is already overbought or underbought as consolidation and profit booking can take place. While you look at these factors, you would also like to consider the fact whether the stock is undervalued or overvalued as that would also have an impact on its escalation and fall.

Stocks with High Market Anticipation

These stocks are the newsmakers, and they would be riding a wave. Their movements are hard to predict as more than the fundamentals and technical aspects; they are running on the market sentiments. Anyway, these stocks can also give you short trading opportunities. However, you must keep in mind that quick in and out of such stocks is always the best. Do not try to hold your position for too long as they can take a serious turn on any side, and you can get locked in them.

From Your Niche

Finally, pick the stocks from your niche. As a new trader, it always feels better to have an open field. However, as you grow in the stock market, you'll realize that having a niche is always a better and more reliable option. Look for all these qualities in the stocks from your field, and you will have very few things to worry about.

CHAPTER - 10

UNDERSTANDING PASSIVE INCOME

Options are perfectly capable of providing you with passive income, but what is passive income really? People seem to think that passive income is easy money, and in some ways it is. However, the term easy misleads most people to think that passive income doesn't involve any work. This is not the truth at all.

So let's begin by defining and taking a look at passive income.

Passive income

There are, broadly speaking, two ways of making money. The first is to exchange your time for money, and the second is to exchange your money for money. The first way is to undertake something like a job or to freelance. You're investing your time in a project and, in return, you get paid. Yes, you're really getting paid for a result if you're freelancing, but my point is that it takes time to produce that result.

The more time you spend on such tasks, the more your earning ability is. If you're a freelance writer, for example, the greater the number of high-quality words you produce, the more you're going to get paid per month. Thus, one of the important things to note about this sort of income is that when you go to sleep, so does your income stream.

When asked about one of the key things that rich people do that poor people don't, Bill Gates responded by saying that the rich leverage their time a lot better (Bodnar, 2017). What does leveraging time mean? Well, Gates' point was that the only thing that is truly limited in our lives is time. We cannot get back the time we've lost, no matter how much we would like to believe that time machines exist.

So ultimately, being financially successful comes down to how well you manage your time. The fact of the matter is that a rich person manages to get paid more for a unit of their time than a poor person does. So how do you get paid more per hour?

Leveraging time

One easy way is to upskill yourself. Simply learn a higher skill and work in a more lucrative field. However, even this doesn't fully leverage your time since once you go to sleep; your money tap is switched off. Hence, the thing to do is to create multiple streams of income. If you have two streams of income paying you at the same time, you can double your hourly wage.

The problem is that you can only do so much at once. You can't perform two jobs at the same moment of time. So what you really want is another source of income that doesn't place demands on your time, which will detract you from your job or hourly source of money. This is precisely what a passive income stream is.

Passive streams leverage your time by simply providing you with an additional amount of money for no additional input of time. I want to make something clear at this point; you will need to spend time creating and maintaining the passive income stream. My point is that your earning ability with this stream doesn't directly depend on how many hours you put into it.

If you spend five hours writing, you're going to get paid for the words you produced in those five hours. If you spend five hours on a passive income stream, you're not going to get paid for those five hours necessarily. You could get paid less; you could get paid more, who knows? The point is that whatever comes, adds to your income as long as you spend the time to do things correctly.

For example, a savings account provides you with passive income. A real estate investment on which you earn rent provides you with passive income. You can spend ten hours a day maintaining your property or spend two hours, it doesn't matter. It will earn you the market level of rent as long as things are maintained properly. There is an aspect of marginal utility with passive income, as economists call it (Bloomenthal, 2019).

Marginal utility refers to the return you receive, in satisfaction or dollars, for every unit of work spent. So if you spend five hours fixing the taps that is probably going to make you good money. Spending an additional hour figuring out which exact shade of white the walls needs to be painted with is probably not going to make you much. Hence, the marginal utility of the former is a lot higher than the latter.

All passive income streams have a level of maximum marginal utility before the returns start dropping off. Trading options, if you're catching on, is subject to the same forces. Remember that your return is measured not just in money, but also in the satisfaction and quality of life you receive

A good way of understanding the value you'll receive and checking which style of trading you wish to adopt is to understand the styles of trading themselves. This way, you can make an accurate judgment of what suits you best.

Active and passive trading

As far as the SEC is concerned, all trading is active. Passive actions are reserved for the investment world. Whatever the good folk of the SEC might think, in reality, there are active forms of trading as well as passive forms. The diversity of the markets means that there exist many ways in which you can divide trading activity. Active versus passive simply happens to be one method of doing so.

Active trading refers to what you think traders actually do. This is where people sit glued to their terminals waiting on tenterhooks for news items to be released and then acting like hotshots when they make money. All of this is accurate except for that last bit, which is a caricature. Either way, active trading usually involves taking directional bets on the market and usually hedging that with some other financial instrument.

Institutional traders, the kinds that trade for hedge funds, big banks and proprietary trading firms (prop shops), are all active traders. No matter what sort of strategies they employ and no matter which instruments they trade, they're always in touch with the markets. They need to be this way because their objective is to squeeze every ounce of money available.

In order to do so, they have to follow the market's every move. They need to know the market backward and cannot have things sneak upon them. What's more, they need to deal with unexpected things that happen over holidays or weekends. For example, as of this writing, oil traders around the world have had to deal with the repercussions of a couple of Saudi Arabian oil fields being attacked.

This happened over the weekend and when the markets were closed. As they returned to work on Monday, you can bet that none of them had slept through the weekend. Active traders tend to look at this sort of thing as an opportunity. Market mispricings happen during such events, and opportunities present themselves. One needs to love the adrenaline rush that occurs during such times. It's no surprise then that, at big banks, the average trader spends about five years on a desk before moving into a managerial position where they supervise other traders who ultimately place all the bets.

It just isn't easy keeping up with such a lifestyle,

after all. In contrast to this active trader, we have the passive trader. The passive trader's returns are not comparable to the active ones. This doesn't mean they make less money, just that they make less than the average active trader.

The tradeoff is that they get to spend their time doing something else. Understandably, a lot of big banks look down upon this sort of thing since a good quality of life on the trading desk usually means losses. However, some hedge funds and other private institutions welcome this sort of thing actively.

You see, a holy grail in the financial world is the pursuit of market neutral-returns. Market neutral means that the strategy makes money no matter what the market does. In such strategies, a trader sets things up via complex financial instruments and then lets the market play itself out. This doesn't mean they go to sleep after this; they simply recycle the strategy in as many markets as possible.

Thus, while the strategy is passive, the trader is active by choice in such institutions. There are sole traders who fix their level of activity within prop shops by trading this way. There is a lot of freedom in such strategies since the trader is not chained to their desk out of necessity. They can vary their involvement in the market, and while the returns don't compare to active strategies, the overall payoff is worth it to the trader.

Almost every passive strategy involves the use of options. The ones that don't involve the usage of derivatives that behaves like options.

Pros and cons of passive income

While there seem to be a lot of positives from passive income, I must warn you that it isn't all a bed of roses. Even roses have thorns, after all. The negatives that lend themselves to passive income almost entirely have to do with how people approach it. A lot of people think that this is lazy money and that things run on autopilot.

Well, this is not the case at all. Every passive income stream, including the ones to do with trading, requires an investment of either time or money or both. In the case of passive trading income, you need to invest in both. Time is needed to learn and study the markets and to develop your skills.

CHAPTER - 11

OPTIONS ON INDEX FUNDS

Buying options on exchange-traded funds is not without risk. However, it can be a little more predictable than doing it for individual stocks. That is because you are simply betting on the direction of the stock market or the price of some major index rather than tracking the fortunes of an individual company.

One of the most popular index funds that are used is called SPY, namely for the S&P 500.

For those who don't know, an exchange-traded fund is basically a mutual fund that trades like a stock. Investment companies collect a large amount of money, and then they buy shares in multiple companies. So, in the case of SPY, the fund owns shares in all 500 companies on the index. A large amount of money has to be assembled to make those kinds of investments.

Try and imagine if you wanted to invest in every single company that belongs to the S&P 500 or the Dow Jones industrial average. That would be quite a daunting task, and unless you are a billionaire, it might even be impossible. But you could imagine trying to buy shares in each individual stock. Let's stick with the S&P 500 as an example. That would mean that you would have to pick out the 500 companies and buy shares in each one of them. Chances are not good for you to get very far in this task.

And then you have to take into account that this is not a static list of companies. That is, it will be changing with time. Companies can be removed from the list, and new ones added as up, and coming corporations replace others.

Another factor to consider would be that you really would not know the best ways to distribute your money among the different stocks even if you had enough to invest in all 500 companies. Usually, investments are weighted so that performance can be improved, as the idea is to beat the market. For this reason, it would be difficult for you, as an individual, to determine how to get the most growth out of your investments.

Therefore, it makes sense to leave such a project to professionals who have a lot of money to invest. So far, it sounds like I have made a great argument for a mutual fund. And I suppose that mutual funds do have their advantages. For starters, we know that such funds automatically give you a diverse portfolio. Also, a professional money manager would attempt to build a portfolio with a higher probability of success, there would be a possibility that his or her fund would actually perform better than the S&P 500 index itself. This is, in fact, what professional money managers try to attempt with these funds. Instead of putting equal investments in each of the S&P 500 companies, what they will do is put a little bit more money in high growth companies and a little bit less in companies that are stable or even in decline.

Of course, while mutual funds have their advantages for people that are planning for retirement and so forth, they might be boring for people who are inclined to be traders rather than safety-oriented long-term investors. And there is a good reason for this. One thing to note about mutual funds is that they don't trade on the stock market. They only trade once a day after the market close. Also, mutual funds are well-known for having high expenses. In fact, in case you didn't know, the expenses associated with mutual funds are a bit notorious if they have loads.

Exchange-traded funds were developed with the idea of taking the advantages of mutual funds but without the disadvantages. So, the first major difference between an exchange-traded fund and a mutual fund is that the exchange-traded fund is traded actively on the stock market. This is a book about options, of course, so we are not going to get into all of the details of why that matters. However, consider the following scenario. Exchange-traded funds trade just like a stock during the day.

So, if the S&P 500 index was going up strongly, you could check the price of the exchange-traded fund, and you may want to get into action. This way, you could buy your shares there and then, or at the right moment as the case may be. But you cannot do this in quite the same way for a mutual fund. You could go ahead and submit an order during the day, but your order won't execute until the mutual fund trades at the end of the day. That means you really cannot be sure what price you are going to get. In contrast, an investor buying shares in an exchange-traded fund knows the exact price, just like anyone buying stock live does.

The second major advantage for exchange-traded funds over mutual funds is that they have very low expenses in comparison. So, the cost of investing in an exchange-traded fund as compared to a mutual fund that tracks the same index is going to be a lot lower.

For these reasons, many exchange-traded funds have become very popular. This is an excellent way for people to invest with diversification. So rather than having to deal with some fancy mutual fund with a bunch of polished publications, that are supposed to make you feel good about all the fees that they are charging you, you can simply sign on to your brokerage account and buy shares of an exchange-traded fund whenever you feel like it.

The popularity of these exchange-traded funds has had a big impact on options as well. Before the advent of exchange-traded funds, the only thing you could do with options was to buy them for regular stocks, but nowadays, you can buy options in all kinds of different ways and for different types of investments. One of the most popular is the SPY, which we mentioned earlier. If you look at the SPY options, the level of activity, as reflected in the volume and open interest, is quite large when compared to that for individual stocks.

You may remember the small numbers that we saw with the Microsoft call options. To make a comparison, now looking at calls that expire in two weeks for SPY, we can see that it is slightly out of the money call option had a volume of 13,969 and an open interest of 19,963. That just gives you an idea of the level of activity associated with the options surrounding this exchange-traded fund. There are a lot of people that are trading these options as compared options trading for a lot of regular stocks. There is a good reason for this, and, for you, it means more liquidity, which helps you get in and out of a trade quickly.

When you are buying and selling options in this case, what you are doing is simply betting on the direction that the S&P 500 will go. Now that will not save you from making the wrong bets from time to time. No matter what, investing is always risky. And when you are talking about the stock market indices themselves, they are going to be more sensitive to external events, such as the government slapping on a new tariff, or if some political event causes an uproar.

This said, remember that with options, one of the advantages is that we can find profit no matter which way the index moves.

Another great thing about the SPY is that the prices are relatively affordable. The share price of the index fund at the writing time is around $289 dollars a share. This is actually quite a nice price point. So, it is roughly about 10% of what the S&P 500 index is.

It is a good price point because higher prices make it easier to make profits. To make profits on low priced stocks like AMD, you have to buy more options, which mean less liquidity. At the other end of the spectrum, we have brands like Amazon, which of course, is quite expensive, even for options.

So, let's look at a slightly out of the money option that expires in two weeks, so that we can get an idea of what the prices are going to be if we decided to purchase an option. A $289 strike call option, which is slightly out of the money, is priced at $1.53. If you remember that options are a hundred shares, which is the price per share, so we could buy this option for $153.

This is a good strategy for when the market is going up. Small changes can mean big money. I, myself, made a recent trade buying some slightly out of the money call options for this exchange-traded fund, SPY. I happened to purchase these options right before a major government announcement related to the general state of the economy. It turned out to be good news, which was pretty much expected, but the actual value was a lot better than what people thought it was going to be. This led to what turned out to be a fairly modest rally in the stock market. Basically, the price of SPY went up by a couple of dollars. If you had 100 shares of SPY, you made a little bit of money. By owning options, however, you would earn $200 per option contract, as I did.

This is a true story, and I hope it encourages you. But, of course, I must warn you that the situation above is far from typical. Nonetheless, those kinds of moves are definitely possible when you are talking about an index fund such as this one. It can happen with company options as well, of course. If Apple, for example, had a surprising earnings report that was upbeat and positive, the price of Apple options would probably make a move of a couple hundred dollars.

But one thing about exchange-traded funds that are tracking major indices is that there is more opportunity for things like this to happen. Any good news that comes out about virtually anything that could impact the economy can drive price changes.

CHAPTER - 12

CANDLESTICKS

When you are engaging in options trading, you do not have to become an expert on stock charts the way that a day trader of stocks needs to be. However, it is a good idea to get some familiarity with the tools of trading so that you can make reasonably sound estimates of where a stock price is moving, which will translate into more winning trades for the options trader.

Also, as an options trader, as we mentioned above, you do not necessarily need to dive deeply into this subject, and you also do not need to be sitting at your computer staring at graphs and charts all day long. Most options traders are simply going to go with the flow of where stock prices are moving, rather than trying to get into the weeds of every last detail.

One reason for this is that changes in share prices are magnified through options. A change of a few tens of cents or dollars is big for the options trader but less significant for a stock trader. Second, a day trader is looking to make their profits over a few hours, so they have to sit there staring at their computer screens waiting for the exact moment to enter and exit a trade, and they can't risk holding the kinds of positions they take overnight. As an options trader, despite the reputation for risk and complexity that comes along with options, you are not going to be trading with the same constraints.

That said, knowing something about the technical analysis can help you be a more successful options trader. It will help you spot changing trends in prices and recognize the right times to enter and exit trades. Of course, this is more art than science, and there is no exact right time to do anything in the stock market, you are just playing your odds. That said, having the knowledge to recognize likely shifts in pricing trends can help you make better trades.

The first main tool that is used by traders to understand and predict changes in pricing trends is the candlestick chart. We are going to look at candlestick chart basics and give you enough information so that you can read candlestick charts and understand them fairly well, and so that you can recognize likely changes in pricing trends. But don't get fooled into magical thinking by candlestick charts, they are not scientific or foolproof. Use them as a guide, not as something absolute that you must follow.

We are also going to look at some of the main tools used in so-called technical analysis. These are mathematical tools that are built to help traders get more information out of pricing trends in the markets. The tools of technical analysis should be viewed as aids as well, and far too many people get fooled into thinking they are infallible, rather than recognizing them for what they are, which is to assist, not absolute, and "true" answers.

The best approach to be taken is to combine a few tools. What most traders do is look for an indication in one of their main ways to track stock market price changes, and then they will use another tool to either confirm or deny what they saw in the first place. Only when two or three different tools or indicators confirm the same pricing trend, do they take action in the markets.

As an options trader – you are going to be applying these tools to the pricing of the underlying stock and not to the option itself. So, if you are interested in trading options on Facebook, you are going to be studying the trading behavior of the Facebook stock, and not the options. When you see favorable changes in the Facebook stock, then you will go ahead and make moves with your options trades.

Candlestick Charts

A candlestick chart is a method of plotting financial data that tells you how prices moved over a given trading session. Rather than having a continuous curve, the price data is broken down into different time frames. There is not a specific time frame that is used; you can create candlestick charts using various time frames. For example, you can have a chart break up a trading day into fifteen-minute increments. Then, the candlesticks will be created for each fifteen-minute increment throughout each trading day, and it will give you pricing information for each of those increments. You can break prices down by the minute, by five-minutes, by an hour, by four hours, and so on.

When you are looking for the right time to enter and exit trades once you have decided that it is about the right time to do so, you might use one minute or five-minute intervals. This will also depend on how active trading is. If a stock is moving by a lot, over a few minutes, options prices can change drastically. So if you have a call option on Netflix in your portfolio, and you are looking to sell it, if prices of the underlying stock are moving by a significant amount, you are going to want to keep close tabs on short term pricing changes. So you might use a five-minute candlestick chart for this purpose.

Candlestick charts are quite general in their application. They can be used for any financial asset that is traded in real-time. They were originally developed in Japan, to track changes in the price of rice. So, they can be used for commodities, stocks, bonds, Forex, or any other asset. Naturally, they are used for stocks.

Looking at the basic unit of a candlestick chart, which is a trading session of the selected time length, the first thing to look at is the color. At a glance, the color of a candlestick tells you the direction of price movement in that trading session. There are different color schemes used on charts, but for stocks, it is typical to use a white background. If the price of the stock went up over the period, then the color is going to be green. If the price of the stock dropped over the period, the color is going to be red.

The candlestick is going to have a "body" and "wicks" coming out of it (in some treatments, the wicks are referred to as "shadows"). The length of the body tells you how much the price moved throughout the entire trading session. This information is to be taken in conjunction with the color of the candlestick.

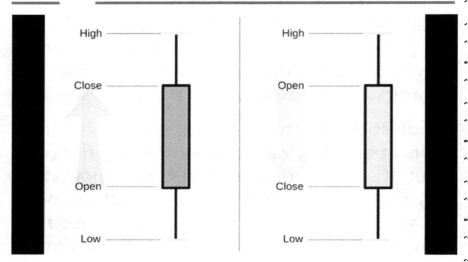

If the candlestick is green, then the bottom of the candlestick is the opening price for the trading session (low in value), and the top of the candlestick is the closing price of the trading session (high in value – so the price rose over the trading session).

If the candlestick is red, the relationships are reversed. In this case, the top of the candlestick is the opening price for the trading session. Then, the bottom of the candlestick is going to be the lower, closing price of the trading session, reflecting that the stock lost value over the period.

Red and green candlesticks are also referred to by the mood they represent. If a candlestick is red, the mood is "bearish" since people are getting out of the stock, and so it can be referred to as a bearish candlestick. Conversely, if the mood is bullish, prices are rising, and people are trying to buy into the stock, and so, a green candlestick is bullish.

The wicks on a candlestick have the same meaning regardless of color. The top wick is the high price attained during the trading session, and the bottom wick is the low price seen during the trading session.

Candlesticks can help you determine the momentum of trading. If the wicks are long, but the body is short, that helps you determine that there was a large push of the price in one direction or another. Still, there was not enough momentum to sustain it, and prices ended up moving back to where they were when the trading session opened, or at least relatively close by.

Remember that pricing is related to supply and demand. So, if prices are rising, there is more demand for the stock. If prices are dropping, people are dumping the stock (increasing the supply), and demand is decreasing.

Candlesticks and Trends

The main way that candlesticks are used is to spot changes in price trends. So, you want to be paying close attention to candlesticks when the stock price has been dropping or rising for some time, and you are looking for signals that a reversal in the price trend is about to occur.

A sudden shift from selling to buying or vice versa is one way that a trend reversal can be noted. This is indicated by an "enveloping" candlestick. That is, you have a candlestick of one type that is larger than the preceding candlestick of the opposite type, then you have a situation where a trend reversal is indicated.

Take, for example, the situation where stock prices have been declining. You are going to see some fluctuation, but there is going to be largely a trend of red candlesticks reflecting the trend of dropping prices. When you see a small red candlestick followed by a bullish candlestick that has a body that is large enough to completely engulf the body of the bearish or red candlestick that preceded it, this is usually a sign that the sell-off is over, and prices are going to start rising. So, this is an indication that you want to buy a call option (or sell a put option) on the stock at this point. When prices are rising, you look for a bearish candlestick to engulf a bullish candlestick to indicate that peak price has been reached, and people are going to start selling off the stock.

Another indicator of a change in trend is when you have seen a trend in one direction, and then you see three candlesticks in a row of the opposite type. Let's consider a downward trend

in prices first. If prices have been dropping, then you see three green or bullish candlesticks in a row, particularly when each succeeding candlestick has a higher closing price, this is a solid indication that prices are going to reverse, and the stock is entering an upward price trend. On the other hand, if you are at the top of an uptrend, and you see three bearish candlesticks in a row, each with lower closing prices than the preceding candlestick, that tells you that the stock price is probably going to start dropping.

Of course, these are rules of thumb; they are not exact or guaranteed to lead to the results described. They often or usually do, but you should confirm these signals using another tool before making major trading decisions.

CHAPTER - 13

THE BEST STRATEGIES TO

MAKE MONEY

Good strategies of any kind of options trading are the major key to any kind of success that is about to be unfolded in any activity. Strategies are normally laid in the trading plan and should be strictly implemented in every options trading move that is likely to be involved. Let us wholly venture into the best strategies so far in options trading.

1. Collars. The collar strategy is established by holding a number of shares of the underlying stock available in the market where protective puts are bought and the call options sold. In this kind of strategy, the options trader is likely to really protect his or her capital used in the trading activities rather than the idea of acquiring more money during trading. This kind is considered conservative and rather much more important in options trading.

2. Credit spreads. It is presumed that the biggest fear of most traders is a financial breakdown.

On this side of strategy, the trader gets to sell one put and then buy another one.

3. Covered calls. Covered calls are a good kind of strategy where a particular trader sells the right for another trader to purchase his or her stock at some strike price and get to gain a good amount of cash. However, there is a specific time that this strategy should be utilized, and in a case where the buyer fails to purchase some of the stock and the expiration date dawns, the contract becomes invalid right away.

4. Cash naked put. Cash naked put is a kind of strategy where the options trader gets to write at the money or out of the money during a particular trading activity and aligning some particular amount of money aside for the purpose of purchasing stock.

5. Long call strategy. This is the most basic strategy in options trading and the one that is quite easy to comprehend. In the long call strategy for options trading, aggressive option traders who happen to be bullish are pretty much involved. This implies that bullish options traders will end up buying stock during the trading activities with the hope of it rising in the near future. The reward is unlimited in the long call strategy.

6. Short call option strategy. The short call

strategy is the reverse of the long call one. Bearish kind of traders is so aggressive in the falling out of stock prices during trading in this kind of strategy. They decide to sell the call options available. This move is considered to be so risky by the experienced options traders believing that prices may drastically decide to rise once again. This significantly implies that large chunks of losses are likely to be incurred, leading to a real downfall of your trading structure and everything involved in it.

7. Long put option strategy. First things first, you should be contented that buying a put is the opposite of buying a call. So in this kind of strategy, when you become bearish, that is the moment you may purchase a put option. Put option puts the trader in a situation where he can sell his stock at a particular period of time before the expiration date is reached. This strategy exposes the trader to a mere kind of risk in the options trading market.

8. Trading time. It is depicted that options trading for a longer period is much value as compared to a short period dating. The longer the trading day, the more skills and knowledge the trader is likely to be engaged into as he or she is likely to get the adequate experience that is needed for good trading.

Mastering good trading moves for a while gives the trader the experience and adequate skills.

9. Bull call spread strategy. In this kind of strategy, the investor gets to purchase several calls at a particular strike price and then purchases the price at a much higher price. The calls always bear a similar expiration date and come from the same underlying stock. This type of strategy is mostly implemented by the bullish options traders.

10. Bear put strategy. This strategy involves a trader purchasing put options at a particular price amount and later selling off at a lower price amount. These options bear a similar expiration date and from the same underlying stock. This strategy is mostly utilized by traders who are said to be bearish. The consequences are limited losses and limited gains.

11. Iron condor. The iron condor involves the bull call spread strategy and the bear put strategy all at the same time during a particular trading period. The expiration dates of the stock are still similar and are of the same underlying stock. Most traders get to use this strategy when the market is expected to experience low volatility rates and with the expectation of gaining a little amount of premium. Iron

condor works in both up and down markets are really believed to be economical during the up and down markets.

12. Married put strategy. On this end, the options trader purchase options at a particular amount of money and, at the same time, get to buy the same number of shares of the underlying stock. This kind of strategy is also known as the protective put. This is also a bearish kind of options trading strategy.

13. Cash covered put strategy. Here, one or more contracts are sold with a 100 shares multiplied with the strike price amount for every particular contract involved in the options trading. Most traders use this strategy to acquire an extra amount of premium on a specific stock they would wish to purchase.

14. Long or short calendar spread strategy. This is a tricky type of strategy. The market stock is said to be stagnant, not moving and waiting for the right timing until the expiration of the front-month is reached.

15. Synthetic long arbitrage strategy. Most traders take advantage of this strategy when they are trying to take advantage of the different market prices in different kinds of markets with just the same property.

16. Put ratio back spread strategy. This is a bearish type of options strategy where the trader gets to sell some put options and gets to purchase more options of just the same underlying stock with a similar expiration date and a lower price.

17. Call ratio back spread. In this strategy, the trader uses both the long and short options positions so as to eradicate consistent losses and target was achieving large loads of benefits over a particular trading period. The essence of this strategy is to generate profits in case the stock prices tend to elevate and reduce the number of risks likely to be involved. This strategy is mostly implemented by bullish kind of options traders.

18. Long butterfly strategy. This strategy involves three parts where one put option is purchased at particular and then selling the other two options at a price lower than the buying price and purchasing one put at even lower prices during a particular trading period.

19. Short butterfly strategy. In this strategy, three parts are still involved where a put option is sold at a much higher price, and two puts are then purchased at a lower price than the purchase price, and a put option is later on sold at a much lower strike price. In both

cases, all put bear the same expiration date, and the strike prices are normally equidistant as revealed in various options trading charts. A short butterfly strategy is the reverse way of the long butterfly strategy.

20. Long straddle. The long straddle is also known as the buy strangle where a slight pull and a slight call are purchased during a particular period before the expiration date reaches. The importance of this strategy is that the trader bears a large chance of acquiring good amounts of profits during his or her trading time before the expiration date is achieved.

21. Short straddle. In this kind of strategy, the trader sells both the call and put options at a similar price and bearing the same expiration date. Traders practice this strategy with the hope of acquiring good amounts of profits and experience limited, various kinds of risks.

22. Owning positions that are already in a portfolio. Most traders prefer purchasing and selling various options that already hedge existing positions. This kind of strategy method is believed to incur good profits and incur losses too in other occurrences.

23. Albatross trade strategy. This kind of strategy aims at gaining some amounts of profits when the market is stagnant

during a specific options trading period or a pre-determined period of time. This kind of strategy is similar to the short gut strategy.

24.   Reverse iron condor strategy. This kind of strategy focuses on benefiting some profits when the underlying stock in the current market dares to make some sharp market trade moves in either direction. Eventually, a limited amount of risks are experienced and a limited amount of profits during trading.

25.   Iron butterfly spread. Buying and holding four different options in the market at three different market prices is involved in the trading market for a particular trading period.

CHAPTER - 14

POSITION ANALYSIS

Swing trading is an approach based on the observation that stock prices never evolve linearly. An increase never takes shape in some time, and it is often punctuated by corrective phases. As per the experts, the basic trading philosophy can be summarized as follows:

- The best opportunities lie in detecting low-risk entry points in the direction of the prevailing trend. Thus, in an uptrend, the trader will have to wait for a correction or consolidation before positioning himself for the purchase.

- Conversely, in a downward trend, the trader will have to position himself only after a rebound around a significant resistance.

In the 1980s, a hedge fund manager went in the same direction by making famous the concept of contraction/expansion. It highlights the NR7 (or smaller range of the last seven days) and specifies that a consolidating market should accelerate just after the appearance of NR7.

Wilder and Appel are the two most cited authors for technical indicators. They introduced mathematics in technical analysis through the development of some technical indicators, very popular in trading rooms.

These indicators are based on different mathematical formulas inspired by physics. The main thesis of these authors is that the speed of an object thrown in the air is reduced as and when its progression, to become zero on the tops. They argue that market movements can be anticipated through these indicators, whose main function is to take the pulse of the market and answer the question: "The current trend—is it intact or exhausting?"

These first steps have been relayed in the

financial world and are the cause of the emergence of technical analysis and many technical indicators of development. People have always been fascinated by the world of trading, however with the risks involved, it can get to be a daunting task. Understanding the stock market and paying attention to the different kinds of trading options can be very stressful. This book will help you understand the basics of swing trading and how you can benefit from it.

Diversification and the Choice of Markets

Diversification is a common-sense concept, which consists of not putting all your eggs in one basket. In our opinion, this approach applies mainly to traders who have a swing trading perspective (medium and long term) but do not seem suitable for short-term traders such as day traders and scalpers. The latter generally focus on a few titles or contracts that they master perfectly and on which they play low amplitude movements.

The Importance of Diversification

The risk of high bankruptcy in trading requires any operator to aim first and foremost the protection of its capital, and in this perspective to ensure that the risks are limited. At any moment, an unexpected event can make him lose a big part of his capital. (Crash, warning on results, extremely negative news).

The concept of diversification is based on the idea that any market operator can be mistaken about the evolution of the markets. Diversification is a way to reduce the risk of error by betting on several uncorrelated contracts rather than relying on a single contract. Some opportunities seem more promising than others and will encourage traders to increase their exposure significantly. Should we increase its exposure excessively on this type of opportunity? Is it reasonable?

After determining the desired global exposure (10%, 5%, 2%), the trader will have to divide his capital in different positions. However, it is possible to allocate the same amount (in the capital and in maximum loss) for each position initiated. The main criticism of this approach is that it assumes that all operations present similar opportunities, which is rarely the case.

Finally, another important element is the correlation between the different securities in the portfolio. Two titles are positively correlated if their evolution is similar. Generally, securities in the same sector move in the same direction. A trader who has highly correlated securities in his portfolio is, therefore, exposed to significant risks that only diversification can mitigate by decreasing the volatility of the portfolio.

In return, the trader will have to accept lower performance.

Peer Trading

This technique is used by many hedge funds and traders in the trading room. It offers a way to reduce risk by taking two opposing positions on two positively correlated products (for example, shares in the same sector). The purpose of this operation is to take advantage of the relative difference in the adjustment between the two financial products.

If a trader believes that Peugeot is undervalued compared to Renault, he can buy Peugeot and sell the Renault to take advantage of this temporary valuation gap. Here, the trader will not try to predict whether Peugeot will go up or down, but is based primarily on the relative evolution of Peugeot compared to Renault. Both stocks may fall, but this will have no impact on his performance since the gain on Renault (a title he sells) should be offset by the loss recorded on Peugeot (a title he buys). This transaction considers that the loss will be largely offset by the gain and will generate a profit. The purpose of the spread is to reduce the risk related to a forecast error and to base its decision on the valuation difference between two assets.

The advantage of this approach is that the trader

is not a victim of market risk - an unexpected rise or fall in the market will have no impact on his position since the loss on an asset (linked to a random event) will be offset by the gain on the other asset assumed to move in the same direction. This technique requires significant funds and low brokerage fees, but it can lead to significant gains for those who control it.

The Limits of Diversification

Diversification reduces the risk associated with trading, but cannot completely eliminate it. Indeed, there is always a portfolio risk that cannot be eliminated despite diversification. In the same way, diversification diminishes the trader's attention and does not allow him to make the most of his positions. This strategy will depend heavily on the fund's philosophy and time horizon. We will privilege for the short term a specialization of the trader on some titles and for the swing traders a specialization in some sectors or markets.

How to Select a Powerful Trading System?

According to J. Welles Wilder, most financial assets evolve in trend 30% of the time. The rest of the time, the markets evolve laterally, that is, no clear trend is detectable. The trader will have to adapt his method to the type of market as well as the current trend. The ideal for a trader is to work in a trending market. Indeed, it is difficult to make money in markets without trend because of brokerage fees and the need for the trader to be constantly in the markets. The trader will have to select first the markets offering the most beautiful configurations, and then make a ranking opportunity offering the best opportunities, according to an order of preference. However, this remark does not apply to traders who favor short-term techniques (day trading and scalping). Good traders will proceed as follows:

Firstly, they will identify several markets trend or about to enter the trend phase; select from those markets with the highest potential and with little or no correlation with others.

Choose one with a high Sharpe ratio. William Sharpe has done a study on the performance of mutual funds in the United States. He put forward the idea that risk-adjusted portfolio return was a significant measure of performance. He created the ratio that bears his name: It goes without saying that it is better to have a smooth performance indicating the regularity of the trader and, therefore, the elimination of the random phenomena of his performance. A chaotic performance means that the investor is subject to significant risk, that its performance may be by chance, and that the risk of ruin is high. A portfolio with a high return and extreme volatility is a danger.

The trader will have to select the trading system with the highest Sharpe ratio. For example, he will be able to analyze a system that he has used in the past and will rely on the history of his performance. He will also be able to evaluate a trading system (not yet used, but derived from his research) thanks to the Sharpe ratio.

A Powerful but Simple Trading System

The trader has every interest in opting for a simple system whose rules he rules, rather than for a more efficient system (on paper) but whose rules are complex.

Indeed, there is a good chance that the trader does not respect his plan, especially with a sophisticated trading system, because his emotions will quickly take over. On the markets, there is no room for hesitation, and it is decisive for a trader to be convinced of the veracity of his system and especially to control it well. To be operational, a system will have to prove its effectiveness in the facts. A system will never be fixed or fixed once and for all, and the trader will proceed by trial and error at first. With experience, the trader can sophisticate his system.

We are convinced that it is preferable to have an imperfect but simpler system rather than a system that is efficient on paper, but complex and, therefore, difficult to implement: the financial markets have the power to destabilize traders, and this deal will have to be imperative. Be taken into account when developing the trading system.

Some Techniques to Improve Its Performance

In this part, we will study the swing trading system, and we will see to what extent it is often successful. We will also study the classic system used by most novice traders, and we will highlight its weaknesses.

The swing trading system means "in the direction of the dominant movement." This system, often used by traders, allows testing the market before increasing its exposure. Indeed, if the market confirms the trader's initial scenario, it is because his reasoning is good, and he can, by crossing some pivotal points, strengthen his position. This system was successfully used by one of the greatest speculators of the last century and is described in his book.

CHAPTER - 15

CHOOSE THE RIGHT MARKET

Understanding the market conditions is crucial as you begin your journey towards becoming a seasoned swing trader.

Patience is crucial in this kind of trading. You will be waiting out for the best prevailing conditions so that you will then move in to close and make profits within a limited period. As such, it then becomes critical that you understand the market conditions that affect the prices of trading. This understanding helps you not just in knowing whether you will make a profit or not, but also in speculating, a significant factor in the trading sector.

To understand market conditions, then, is to strategize on how you will go about your trading venture. In trading, the market moves in what traders call waves, and these waves can be either impulsive or corrective. Sudden surges usually go with the trend, while corrective waves run counter to this, acting to correct the impulse waves. Understanding this, then becomes the key in how you will trade at a given moment.

Trendiness

Trendiness is a critical component of the trading market. In swing trading, they are essential, as you will see to close and make profits within a specified set of times.

This move of identifying and confirming trends is called moving average. Further, you will need to understand a step called the simple moving average (SMA). Here, you will take all the closing prices for a select number of days then add them up. Then, you will receive the total you get and divide it by itself. The answer is the average price of the security exchange.

When you do this over several different select days, it gives an idea of what is happening in the market. This idea will help you understand whether putting in your money on a given trend is worth it.

When you take the time to understand the market, then, when you do your mathematics, the general trend of the market price when you put it in a graph will provide you with how the market is or has been performing through the selected number of days. If the general movement of the chart points upwards, then it shows you that the prices of security are going up. If it looks downwards over the selected period, then the prices are going down, Trend up and trend down.

To further smoothen how the SMA performs, you can enhance it through the exponential moving average (EMA). The EMA provides trends that give details of more recent data, unlike the SMA, which is broader. To determine the current prices, many traders will go with the EMA as it readily lends itself to helping you calculate the more recent rates in the market.

A (n) then stands for the price of the asset at a given period while (n) represents the period and the total number of periods.

As we can see, then, to understand how the market goes, then it is vital that you get to know how trends will affect how you trade and whether you will make a profit or not.

To make money off from trend trading, though, you will need to get in early, then hold your place until the trend reverses. What this then means is that you will need to make a proper assessment that the prices will keep moving in the direction that you want and will not change along the way.

Because of this, the risks of trading off the trend are higher, and thus, you will need to be rigorous in your risk assessment.

However, the higher risk of trend trade means then that you are also likely to make huge profits when it does go right. When you make your move at just the right time, and hold out, you will then reap significantly from it.

Range

In stock trading, the range is the difference between the buying price and the selling price at the highs and lows of the stock market.

Some traders will often attempt to trade within ranges, rather than through following trends, in what is known as range trading. Unlike the trend trader, the range trader does not give much emphasis on the direction of the graph. Their thinking is that, no matter how far the currency falls or rises, since it will most often revert to its natural point, they then place their money on this. So, they make their money by capitalizing on this undulating movement of the prices over and over again.

As we see, this requires a very different type of management from the trend and will need you to be willing to be wrong at the start of the trade. Here, you do not need to assess the market movement. This assessment then allows you to build on the trading position that you got in.

Still, you need to identify the range in your assessment. You will need to identify the points at which the currency has fallen into or risen into at least twice, before recovering. The two locations do not need to be identical, but close to each other and similar.

Therefore, based on this, range trading is one that will generate profits for you, but as with any investment, it comes with its risks, and you will need to be on the lookout.

When you do not intend on trading on the range, you will still need to understand it as it will guide you in making the calculations that come with placing your bet on the stocks. The scale will also allow you to know which currencies you would want to trade-in. Stronger currency pairs often will have shorter ranges, but because of their stability, they will then be close to a guarantee that you will make your profits. They also trade frequently, which then means that you will be able to make cumulative profits from the small margins that the deal offers.

Relative Strength Index

RSI, as many traders call it, is a central unit of assessment in the stock market.

The RSI will be what will help you gain entry into the market. So, what is the relative strength index?

The RSI is an indicator that will help you with looking into the short signals under the presumption that the prices have drastically been oscillating that the market ends up overbought or oversold.

The RSI will be a great companion for you when you begin making your entry into the trading. Because you will need to understand how the market moves, the RSI then provides you will have an opportunity to look into the data and determine how the market is moving.

The RSI, as with many indicators in the trade business, will provide you with details on what trade opportunities are great for you.

However, many trading experts generally agree that you will be better off using the RSI, among other trading technical tools. To know that trade will yield the returns you want, you will need all these indicators to all give you the same or similar data. This result is because, through analyzing the market from different angles, one can then make their choice based on the consistent feed that they receive from the various indicators.

So, this will mean that aside from the RSI, you will also need candlesticks and moving averages, as well as the volumes traded to tell you the whole story. The information does not necessarily have to be within the same day. However, they need to be consistent enough so that they are within the same time frame, such as in a span of one or two, or at most, three days.

However, when you make this trade, understand that trading does not have a complete guarantee that you will make the profits that you so wish to make. As one trader put it "there isn't a magic bullet." You will need to take the risk without having to hold out for too long. As such, these technical analysis tools should only be a guide for you. You will need to put your money into the trade at the end of the day, with all the risks hanging up over your head. As such, the analysis is only part of the deal. You will need to put your hands down and get down to business.

Understand Group of Stock

Group of stocks is the select number of commodities that you keep an eye on as they should be the ones that you have selected to trade. This group of stock will include currencies, gold, and oil, among many others.

Understanding the group of stock will need you always to keep your eyes off the ground, following through the news so that you are well aware of the small changes within. In trading, small changes will often have significant changes, and you will need to continually be mindful so that you do not get checked out and find yourself at a disadvantage.

The changes let you understand the portfolio package and the number of stocks within the box, as well as give you indicators on the charts. Trading will need you to have a clear plan, with it being that when you move in, you will need to have a target and a limit. Then you will need to have the last point of loss you will take before you opt-out of the deal. When you take the time to understand it, you will then stop yourself from impulse buying, which, while it can work out for you sometimes, the fact that it will take you off your plans means that it will often become less of trading and more of gambling.

CHAPTER - 16

BEFORE YOU ENTER A TRADE

Let me stop you right there before you start making trades. There are a few things you need to be aware of before you enter the market; here are the steps you need to go through.

1. Portfolio Balance

Before you do anything, you need to look at your portfolio balance first. When you're planning a new trade, it's always important to ask yourself why you need that trade and how it will affect your portfolio. Do you even really need it? For instance, if your portfolio already has plenty of bearish trades, it would generally be better for you to avoid adding more.

You need to reduce your risk in every situation, so the key here is to balance out your trades. That's how one develops a great portfolio, risk diversification. When you have a bunch of bearish trades in hand, look for bullish trades to offset the risk and vice versa. Once you internalize this, it becomes far easier to focus on what your portfolio really needs and filter out the rest from the very first moment you start looking for a new trade.

2. Liquidity

Liquidity is straight up one of the most important qualities of a good, tradable option. You don't want to be stuck with an illiquid option, no matter how lucrative it looks. Here's a simple rule to follow when looking for a new trade: for it to be a good trade, the underlying stock should be trading at least 100,000 shares daily. If the numbers are less than that, the trade isn't worth your time. In a market as big and efficient as the one we have, the calculations only become more accurate with the passage of time. Similarly, when considering the underlying options, there should be a minimum of 1000 open interest contracts for the strikes you are trading for it to be a good trade.

3. Implied Volatility Percentile

Say, if AAPL has IV of 35%, but IV percentile of 70%, it means that while the current volatility is low, in the last one year, it was higher than what it currently is (35%) for more than 70% of the time. So the implied volatility for AAPL is relatively high, and you should be looking to employ premium-selling strategies.

4. Picking a Strategy

Picking a great strategy is as much a matter of eliminating as it is a matter of selecting, perhaps even more so. You can easily eliminate a bunch of strategies once you have a good idea of the IV and the IV percentile of the underlying stock and how it affects the options. For example, it's easy to eliminate strategies like debit spreads and long single options when you know the IV is high and the pricing rich. Then it's time to consider our risk tolerance and account size to pick the best strategy out of the ones left (iron condors, credit spreads, strangles, etc.)

5. Strikes & Month

Your personal trading style and goals also play a big part in how you decide to pick trades. Some people are more risk-averse than others, and that's okay. You should always select the right strategy based on the risk level you're comfortable with. If you're selling credit spreads, let's say, and you have the option to sell them at either a strike price that has a 90% chance of success of a strike price that has a 65% chance of success, you need to decide which option you want to go with based on the level of aggression you're comfortable with. It needs to fit your trading style and your goals.

6. Future Moves

You must've heard the popular saying that a chess grandmaster can foresee as many as 20 moves ahead. A good options trader also plans ahead and foresees future moves. If you're not thinking a few moves ahead, you're going to lose to the market more often than not. Always have a Plan B in case things go nasty and you need to shield yourself from losses.

Sometimes, you just won't be able to make a winning trade. That's just how the market works; some trades go wrong no matter how well you plan. But you need to keep asking yourself the important questions constantly. When you do this, your mind stays sharp and ready to jump into action to formulate a new plan or make an adjustment as and when the need arises.

Tips for Becoming a Top Tradersuccessful— Trading Strategies

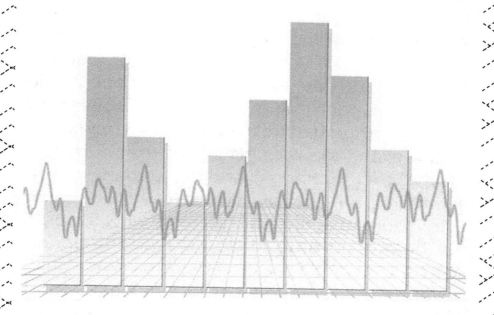

When all is said in done, you are the one responsible for turning your venture into foreign exchange into a successful endeavor. That is actually one of the great things about the stock. You do not have a boss screaming down your neck, telling you to do something that you do not agree with. You have the ability to come up with your own trading plan based on your own research and your own knowledge. That being said, success can come more quickly for some than for others, and a lot of the time, this has to do with approaching this endeavor with the right strategy.

Strategy 1. Buy low and sell high

If you began stock trading today with $25,000 in your pocket and access to a trading platform, all ready and raring to go, how would you know what is low and what is high? It's your first day. Naturally, for you to understand what would represent a good low investment and conversely what is high, you need to have some knowledge of the exchange rate history of that currency. Maybe the exchange rate for Japanese yen seems low, but actually, compared to last year or a few months ago, it's a little high. Now it would not be a good time to buy. Maybe the pound seems low right now, but yesterday the British government announced that the first round of the Brexit negotiations with the EU failed, and, therefore, the pound may have room to go lower than it was when you logged onto your trading platform. Maybe you should wait and see what the pound is later today or tomorrow and buy then. The point here is that buying low and selling high requires understanding the patterns associated with that stock and what might cause it to go up or down. And that's merely the buying side of things. A good plan will prevent you from selling too soon, or even not selling soon enough.

Strategy 2. Focus on not losing money rather than on making money

This may not be an easy strategy to understand initially, in part because not losing money and making money seem like two sides of the same coin. They are, but they are not identical. One of the personality types that is associated with difficulty in finding success in trading is the impulsive type. This type of person wants to make money, and they want to make it quick. They have a vague strategy about how they plan on doing that, but the most important thing to them is that they have a high account balance to make as many trades as they need to turn a profit. This is the wrong approach. Currencies are not the same as stocks. The value of a stock may change very little even after a week's time, so my strategy involves a lot of trades in order to make money is usually not the best strategy.

Strategy 3. Develop a sense of sentiment analysis

Alright, the third strategy was going to be about Fibonacci retracement, which is a type of technical analysis of the market, but as this is the basics of stock trading, we are going to go into a different strategy that is not any easier than a Fibonacci retracement, just different. Sentiment analysis is a term that is used in many different specialties, not just finance, and it is not easy to describe. A key to understanding sentiment analysis is likening it to public opinion. The economy may be booming, people have more money in their pocket, so the stock of this hypothetical country should increase in value, but maybe it doesn't. Maybe there is something that is causing the market to be bearish and which, therefore, might cause the stock to drop. As you perhaps can tell, as this analysis is not based on any concrete information, it can be thought of as intuitive, and no one has intuition on day 1. Let's just be honest about that. Intuition comes from experience. But the purpose of this strategy is to introduce to you the idea that not the foreign exchange market, like any market, is not going to behave like a machine because it's not a machine. Markets are places where human beings come together, and humans are unpredictable, often in a frustrating way.

Research

Regardless of the investment that you make, be sure always to do your research. Doing research is a must. It is what will increase your chances of making the right investment decision. As the saying goes, "Knowledge is power." The more that you understand something, the more likely that you will be able to predict how it will move in the market. This is why doing research is essential. It will allow you to know if something is worth investing in or not. Remember that you are dealing with a continuously moving market, so it is only right that you keep yourself updated with the latest developments and changes, and the way to do this is by doing research.

Remember that gaining information is not limited to just surfing the web for information. It is also suggested that you join online groups and forums that are related to your chosen investment. There is also a good chance that you can learn something from them.

Do not rush the process of doing research. Take note that you make decisions based on the information that you have on hand, and such information that you have will depend on the time and efforts that you put into doing research. Make sure that all of your decisions are backed up by solid research and analysis.

Have a plan

Whether you are going to start forex trading or trade in general, it is always good to have a plan. Make sure to set a clear direction for yourself. This is also an excellent way to avoid being controlled by your emotions or becoming greedy. You should have a short-term plan and a long-term plan. Poor planning leads to poor execution, but having a good idea usually ends up favorably. You should stick to your plan. However, there are certain instances when you may have to abandon your project, such as when you realize that sticking to the same program will not lead to a desirable outcome or in case you find a much better idea. Proper planning can give you a sense of direction and ensure the success of execution.

Make your plans practical and reasonable. Remember that you ought to stick to whatever project you come up with, so be sure to keep your ideas real. Before you come up with an idea, you must first have quality information. Again, this is why doing research is very important.

CHAPTER - 17

OPTION TRADING AND OTHER FINANCIAL INSTRUMENTS

With regards to exchanging and interest, all in all, there are a wide range of money related instruments that can be utilized for potential benefits. A money related instrument is basically any tradable resource, regardless of whether it is money, proof of possession in a substance, different wares or even the authoritative option to get or convey another budgetary instrument.

Stocks are most likely the most popular budgetary instrument, yet there are additionally bonds, prospects, and obviously, choices contracts. There is cash to be produced using putting resources into, or exchanging any money related instrument on the off chance that you comprehend what you are doing.

On the off chance that you are keen on alternatives exchanging, at that point, you clearly need to recognize what choices contracts are and how they work. In any case, it likewise pays to have a comprehension of other budgetary instruments and how they work by methods of examination. Regardless of whether your venture plan includes just exchanging alternatives, it can, in any case, help to discover more about other money related instruments.

You may well choose to adhere to just exchanging alternatives, yet you additionally may conclude that you need to put resources into other money related instruments as well. In this area, we contrast choices with the accompanying monetary instruments:

1. Stocks

2. Bonds

3. Forex

4. Fates

5. Warrants

Contrasts Between Stocks and Options

If you somehow happened to ask how a great many people need to engage in contributing, at that point, the most widely recognized answer would likely purchase stocks in publically recorded organizations. This is generally in light of the fact that purchasing stocks are probably the least difficult approaches to put away cash, and anybody can do it with only a tad of information.

There is unquestionably cash to be produced using purchasing or exchanging stocks, and there various individuals that do precisely that. Notwithstanding, when you contrast exchanging stocks with exchanging choices, there are some unmistakable preferences that alternatives offer.

All things considered, numerous speculators effectively exchange stocks to make bigger returns than is conceivable through utilizing a purchase and hold technique to fabricate a portfolio that just increments in esteem after some time.

Notwithstanding, purchasing and selling stocks isn't the best way to benefit from the money related markets using any and all means, and there are numerous different strategies that can be utilized. Exchanging choices is one specific type of putting that has developed essentially in prevalence: among prepared, master financial specialists, however, with an entire scope of individuals.

Alternatives exchanging is open to anybody, and despite the fact that it's somewhat more mind-boggling than simply purchasing stocks, it isn't that hard for anybody to find out about the subject and get included. One of the primary things you ought to comprehend is the manner by which putting resources into choices is not the same as putting resources into stocks, and on this page we clarify the fundamental contrasts between the two.

Crucial Differences

The principle distinction among stocks and choices is the way that when putting resources into stocks, you are really purchasing a security that can go up or down in esteem, yet when putting resources into alternatives, you are purchasing a subsidiary. A subsidiary is basically an exchanging instrument that gets its incentive from some other security. The estimation of the subordinate is along these lines firmly connected to the estimation of that other security. This is known as the fundamental security, yet it can likewise be influenced by different elements.

On account of alternatives, there are different protections other than stocks; it can likewise be other money related instruments, for example, items and monetary standards. The truth of the matter is that there is an entire scope of various sorts of alternatives that can be purchased and sold methods you can estimate on a wide assortment of money related instruments when exchanging choices.

At the point when you purchase stocks in a specific organization, you are really purchasing an offer in that organization. In the event that the organization performs well, at that point, the odds are that your venture will increment in worth, and there are two manners by which you can make an arrival. To begin with, you can decide to sell at a greater expense than you purchased to arrive at a higher benefit. Second, on the off chance that the organization you have put resources into is gainful, at that point, they may grant investors with a yearly profit (a portion of those benefits that is paid to any individual who holds stock in the organization).

It's conceivable to make awesome returns by holding profit paying stocks for an extensive stretch of time, you despite everything, own the real resource that you can decide to sell whenever. You can likewise decide to short sell stocks in an organization and cause a benefit on the off chance that they go down in esteem.

How alternatives work is extraordinary; when you purchase investment opportunities, you are purchasing an agreement that gives you the option to purchase or sell explicit stocks at a concurred cost. While these agreements arrive in a wide range of classifications, they would all be able to be classed as either calls or puts. Calls give you the option to purchase a particular stock at a fixed value (this fixed cost is known as the strike cost) while puts give the option to sell a particular stock at a fixed cost.

On the off chance that you purchase calls, the value you pay for them doesn't get you any real stock; it essentially gives you the option to get it.

Favorable Circumstances of Options Over Stocks

Perhaps the greatest favorable position of purchasing brings over purchasing stock is the way that you can confine potential misfortunes while as yet profiting by potential benefits. You should put resources into a specific organization, for instance, that had a high possibility of expanding altogether in esteem, yet additionally had a little danger of falling essentially in esteem. On the off chance that you purchased the stock, you would profit by any ascent in esteem, however, you would likewise be presented to any fall in esteem.

For instance, suppose these stocks were exchanging at $20, and you chose to purchase 1,000 offers. If they went up to $30, you could sell your 1,000 offers for a benefit of $10 each. This would give you a sum of the $10,000 benefit. In this way, any commissions you caused for your exchanges would simply be a special reward to your benefit. Be that as it may, if they tumbled to $10 before you chose to cut your misfortunes, you would lose $10,000.

Presently assume you had chosen to purchase call alternatives on the stock rather, and you purchased 1,000 calls at $1 each, giving you the option to purchase 1,000 offers at the strike cost of $20.

On the off chance that the stock tumbled to $10, at that point, you would just not practice your alternative, and you would just have lost the $1,000 you initially contributed. This model shows that even though you may forfeit a little level of your benefits if the value moves as arranged, you are enormously diminishing your presentation to chance if the value moves the other way.

This model likewise features another significant favorable position of alternatives overstocks, and that is influence. To claim the 1,000 offers at $20 in the above model, you would have needed to contribute $20,000. Expecting the value rose as featured for a benefit of $10,000, this would give you a half profit for your speculation.

In any case, purchasing the 1,000 choices at $1 would have implied a venture of just $1,000. With the offers ascending to $30 and an absolute benefit of $9,000, you would get an 800% profit for your speculation. Not exclusively can purchasing alternatives limit your hazard. Yet, it can likewise give you the potential for a lot more prominent return comparative with your underlying venture.

This fairly fundamental model ought to furnish you with a thought of how exchanging alternatives can be a helpful method to contribute. Various ways exchanging choices can be utilized, including supporting a current position contingent upon what systems you wish to use.

CHAPTER - 18

SIGNIFICANT DIFFERENCES BETWEEN FUTURES AND OPTION TRADING

The essential contrast, among alternatives and prospects is in the commitments of the gatherings in question. The holder of a choices contract has the option to purchase the primary resource at a fixed cost, however, not the commitment. The essayist, or dealer of the agreement, is committed to sell the holder the hidden security (or get it) if the holder chooses to practice their choice.

This clearly puts the holder of an agreement at a favorable position, in such a case that the hidden security moves against them, they can just allow the agreement to lapse and not acquire any misfortunes far beyond the first expense. On the off chance that the fundamental security moves the correct way for the holder (and in this way against the author), at that point, the essayist must respect their commitment.

In a fates contract, the two gatherings are obliged to satisfy the provisions of the agreement at the purpose of lapse. This is an exceptionally noteworthy contrast. Purchasing a prospects contract where you will be obliged to purchase a specific security at a fixed value conveys considerably more hazard than purchasing an alternatives contract where you reserve the privilege to purchase a specific security at a fixed cost, yet are not obliged to proceed with it if that security neglects to climb in an incentive as you anticipate. The two gatherings associated with a fates contract are viably presented to boundless obligation.

The costs included are likewise extraordinary. At the point when an alternative contract is first composed, its essayist offers it to the purchaser and gets the cash that the purchaser pays. Contingent upon the provisions of the agreement, the underlying security included, and the conditions of the essayist, the author may must have a specific measure of edge close by. They may likewise be required to top up that edge if the underlying security moves against them. Nonetheless, the purchaser possesses those agreements out, and out and no further supports will be required from them.

With prospects, however, as the two gatherings are presented to misfortunes contingent upon what direction the cost of the hidden security moves, they are both required to have a specific measure of edge close by. Value contrasts on fates are settled day by day, and either gathering could be dependent upon an edge call if the estimation of the fundamental security has moved against them. This contributes to a great extent to why the fates exchanging is commonly viewed as more dangerous than choices exchanging. Beneath, we take a gander at several points of interest, exchanging alternatives brings to the table.

Points of Interest of Options Over Futures

As referenced above, when exchanging fates, you are conceivably presented to large misfortunes whichever side of the agreement you are on. In the event that you have the commitment to purchase hidden security at a fixed cost and the security moves fundamentally over that fixed value, at that point, you could lose free totals. On the other hand, on the off chance that you have the commitment to sell a fundamental security at a fixed cost and the security moves altogether beneath that fixed value then you could encounter sizable misfortunes.

On the off chance that you are composing alternatives agreements and assuming a commitment to either purchase or sell hidden security at a fixed value, at that point, you are presented to comparable dangers. Be that as it may, you can exchange choices only by purchasing contracts and not keeping in touch with them. This implies you can constrain your potential misfortunes on every single exchange you make to the measure of cash you put resources into purchasing explicit agreements.

At whatever point you purchase choices gets, the most dire outcome imaginable is that they terminate useless and you lose your underlying speculation. Regardless of whether you would like to compose contracts notwithstanding getting them, you can undoubtedly make spreads to guarantee that your misfortunes are constrained continuously. The potential for restricted liabilities in choices exchanging is a significant preferred position, especially for those that are against high hazard ventures.

Another huge favorable position alternatives exchanging offers is adaptability. There are various systems that you can use to make spreads that empower you to benefit from multi-directional value developments. For instance, you could make a spread that would bring about benefit if the necessary security went down in esteem a smidgen, or on the off chance that it remained stable, or on the off chance that it went up in an incentive by any sum. This would possibly bring about restricted misfortunes if the fundamental security went down a critical sum.

With prospects contracts, you can commonly just bring in cash from the fundamental security moving the correct way for you. There could be great misfortunes if your speculation moves off course or if a fair outcome happens.

Contrasts Between Warrants and Options

Bunches of budgetary instruments are totally not the same as one another, while many are actually very comparable. Warrants and choices are two monetary instruments that are similar in many regards, which regularly prompts financial specialists and merchants to accept they are about something very similar. While they do share numerous qualities, there are two or three critical contrasts between the two which are imperative to perceive.

Choices contracts are on an elementary level not quite the same as most other monetary instruments, but then numerous individuals do, in any case, get choices exchanging mistook for different types of exchanging, for example, forex exchanging or stock exchanging.

Of all the money related instruments that can be exchanged on trades and markets the world over, it's really warrants that are the most like alternatives. On this page, we give data on how warrants work and how they are unique in relation to alternatives. We likewise take a gander at a portion of the points of interest that we accept choices offer.

Significant Differences Between the Two

Warrants and choices are fundamentally the same as, and they are frequently viewed as basically something very similar yet just with an alternate name only like stocks and offers are necessarily the equivalent. In any case, there are contrasts between the two, and it's significant that you perceive these distinctions and what they mean for the financial specialist. Despite the fact that they share a lot of similar qualities, there two or three critical parts of warrants that make them very particular from choices.

The meaning of an alternatives agreement can be streamlined as follows: a monetary agreement that concedes the holder the right, yet not the commitment, to either purchase or sell an underlying security at a concurred cost by a lapse date. These agreements can be named either calls, which give the holder the option to purchase the primary security, or puts which give the holder the option to sell the fundamental security.

In their run of the mill structure, warrants are fundamentally the same as European style call choices, in that they give the holder the option to purchase hidden security at a fixed cost on a fixed lapse date. Be that as it may, alternatives contracts are ordinarily composed by either private speculators or market creators, and the fundamental security can be a wide assortment of money related instruments. Warrants, in any case, are composed by organizations with the hidden security being stock in the giving organization.

So in spite of the fact that the essential rule of the two money related instruments is fundamentally the same as there is a vast contrast as far as who is composing the agreement. While most alternatives follow a specific normalized system, warrants are basically redone accurately to suit the giving organization and what they are attempting to accomplish.

For instance, while the length of choices are estimated in months, warrants can be, and regularly are, estimated in years and will, in general, have an any more extended life expectancy. Due to the way that they are exceptionally tweaked, warrants are commonly exchanged over the counter markets as opposed to the publically exchanged trades.

Warrants are given by organizations for an assortment of reasons; they are regularly connected to bonds so as to make the bonds an increasingly alluring choice for speculators. They can likewise be joined to favored stocks and can even be utilized in special value bargains. One of the other fundamental contrasts is that practiced alternatives dependent on stock include the deal and acquisition of existing stock, while practiced call warrants bring about the organization giving new portions of stock.

Points of Interest of Options Over Warrants

Regardless of the likenesses between the two instruments, the distinctions that exist loan specific points of interest to utilizing alternatives in an exchanging system as opposed to warrants. Perhaps the most compelling motivation to exchange alternatives is the capacity to make spreads, which can be utilized for various purposes. These spreads can be made in various manners, yet they usually include all the while purchasing and composing alternatives contracts.

While warrants can, in any case, speak to a keen interest in their own right, there are fundamentally less exchanging methodologies that can be utilized, including warrants than those including alternatives. Likewise, as they are commonly exchanged over the counter, they are not as simple to purchase and sell as choices contracts. They are, to a great extent, exchanged on the trades and, in this way, significantly more available.

Since warrants are composed distinctly by organizations whose own stock is the fundamental security, or by a monetary establishment speaking to that organization, it's impractical to take a short situation on them and bring in cash from the stock going down in esteem. This decreases the quantity of potential open doors for making benefit.

Contrasted with alternatives that can be utilized to benefit from stock and other monetary instruments going down in an incentive just as up.

In rundown, purchasing warrants can unquestionably be a smart thought in the right conditions, yet choices offer more prominent openness and flexibility to brokers.

CHAPTER - 19

CREDIT SPREAD STRATEGY

When it comes to trading options, a trader has many options spread strategies from which he can choose. A spread refers to the purchase and sale of two or more options that have the same underlying asset to take advantage of opportunities at both ends of a trade.

Spreads are classified in different ways, A credit spread, also called a net credit spread, is a spread strategy that has to do with the net receipts of premiums while a debit spread is one that involves net premium payments.

When creating a credit spread, the trader sells or writes a high-premium option and, at the same time, buys an option with a low premium. The premium that the trader receives from writing the option is often more significant than the premium he pays to get the low-cost option. The difference is credited to the seller's trading account. When traders use the credit spread strategy, the maximum amount they receive, the one that is credited to their account when the position is entered, is called the net premium.

Looking at an example, let's say a trader takes up the credit spread strategy and writes a November call option whose strike price is $25 for $2, then simultaneously buys another November call option whose strike price is $30 for $1. Taking the usual multiplier, 100 shares per stock, then the net premium received will be $100, got from ($200 - $100). The trader will also enjoy more profits if the spread narrows.

When a trader is bearish, he is hopeful that the stock prices will go down, and he opts for extended call options with a strike price before proceeding to sell a short all option within the same class, at a lower strike price. A bullish trader is often optimistic that the price of the underlying stock will go up and opts to buy call options at a strike price before proceeding to sell an equal number of call options at a higher strike price. The call options must be of the same class and have the same expiration.

Credit Spread Characteristics

Credit spreads have several unique characteristics with which you can differentiate them from other options trading strategies.

They include:

- Credit Spreads are Useful Risk Management Tools

We noted that traders use spreads as tools to manage risk. Credit spreads enable the traders to limit the risks to which they are exposed substantially by making them forego a limited profit potential. With the spread, traders can calculate the total amount of money they are risking even before they enter a position.

- Credit Spreads Enhance Trading Versatility

Traders can identify a combination of contracts to take either a bearish or bullish position by doing one of two things. First, they have the option of establishing a credit put spread, which is a bullish position whose short put has more premium. Second, traders can choose to create the credit call spread, a spread that takes a bearish position and has more premium on its short call.

Now, let's have an in-depth look at each of the strategies mentioned above:

The Credit Put Spread

Instead of outright selling your uncovered put options, traders take up the credit put spread. You see, selling an uncovered put option is a bullish move that is best taken when you expect the price of the underlying index or stock to go up. Traders sell the uncovered put option to generate income and then wait for the time limit to expire so that the option can be termed worthless. Although the risks involved when traders do this are somewhat limited, they can be substantial. The trader continues to lose money right until the value of the stock falls to zero.

Just like other spreads, the credit spread involves purchasing and selling options contracts simultaneously. Usually, the options are of the same class (whichever puts or calls) and riding on the related underlying security. However, for vertical credit put spreads, the strike prices are different, although the expiration month is similar.

Also note that whenever you take up a bullish position using the credit put spread, the premium you receive for the option sold is higher than the premium you pay for the option. The result is that trading the option generates an income, although the amount will be less than what you would have got had you taken the open call position.

Let's see an example. Suppose you buy 20 Company X March 65 puts each at $1 then sells 20 Company X March 70 puts each at $3, you will have a net credit of $2. In this case, the spread will be executed at $ 4,000 ({$3 premium received - $1 premium paid} * {20 contracts each carrying 100 shares}).

If the market price of Company X shares closes above $67, you will make a profit. However, you will only maximize your profit (at least to get to $4,000) if the shares close at $70 and above. You will end up losing money if Company X's shares price goes below $67. For example, if the price fell to $65 or below, you stand to lose up to $2,000.

Kindly remember that taxes, fees, and commissions, though not included in this example, will affect the outcome of the trade, and ought to be factored in.

A trader would opt to take up this trade with the March 70 puts uncovered. Well, this could have resulted in a higher profit, $2,000, rather than the $1,500 profit received using the credit spread put. However, it is worth risking the $500 because the spread limits the risks involved significantly.

Had you sold the March 70 puts uncovered, primarily, your loss potential could have been a staggering $67,000 ($70,000 spent on buying the stock - $3,000 received on selling the puts), but that would only be if the company X stock value fell all the way to zero.

The credit spread scenario now appears better because under no circumstance can your maximum loss exceed $2,000.

Credit Call Spread

Usually, traders use credit call spreads instead of outright selling uncovered call options. Selling uncovered call options is a bearish trading strategy that traders can use when they expect the value of the security or the index underlying to go down. The goal of taking the credit call spread strategy is to generate income that could have been raised had the trader directly sold the uncovered call option and waited for the option to expire or become worthless.

Whenever you use the credit call spread to open a bearish position, the premium you pay for it will be lower than the premium you will receive once the option is sold. For this reason, the income you will generate using the credit call spread will be less than the income you would have raised had you taken an open position.

The workings of the credit call spread are just like those of the credit put spread except that the loss and profit regions are on opposite sides of the break even point.

CHAPTER - 20

POINTS OF INTEREST OF OPTION TRADING

It's straightforward why purchasing stocks or exchanging them is engaging such a large number of financial specialists; it's generally easy to do, and there is certainly cash to be made.

Alternatives exchanging, specifically, has numerous focal points, and there are a lot of reasons why this type of exchanging is deserving of thought for anybody hoping to contribute. On this page, we take a gander at the primary purposes behind exchanging choices and why it very well may be such a smart thought, regardless of whether it is an increasingly difficult subject with such a long way to go. The accompanying points are secured:

- Capital Outlay and Cost Efficiency

- Hazard and Reward

- Adaptability and Versatility

1. Capital Outlay and Cost Efficiency

Perhaps the best explanation behind exchanging alternatives is the way that it's conceivable to make noteworthy benefits out of doing as such without necessarily needing enormous aggregates of cash. Along these lines, it's optimal for financial specialists with small beginning capital just as those with bigger spending plans. The potential for huge benefits from little ventures is, to a great extent, down to the utilization of influence. In fundamental terms, you can utilize influence to get all the more exchanging power from the capital you have.

This is a to some degree streamlined model, yet it illustrates how you can produce sizable comes back from whatever beginning capital you have access.

2. Hazard and Reward

In sure regards, the hazard versus reward advantage offered by exchanging alternatives is firmly connected to the above point. As the given model appeared, it's conceivable to make proportionately higher comes back from a similar capital venture. We utilized this guide to feature that exchanging should be possible with generally limited quantities of beginning capital, and it very well may be an extremely cost practical approach to contribute. Furthermore, choices exchanging can offer a much improved hazard versus reward proportion if the correct exchanging methodologies are utilized.

It ought to be clarified that there are clearly chances included, in light of the fact that there are with a speculation. Some exchanging systems can be extremely unsafe, in fact, particularly those that are exceptionally theoretical in nature.

3. Adaptability and Versatility

One of the most engaging components of choices is the adaptability that they offer. This is in agreement to most types of detached venture, and even some progressively dynamic structures, where there are restricted methodologies included and constrained approaches to bring in cash.

For instance, on the off chance that you are adopting a purchase and hold strategy to speculation and just purchasing stocks to construct a portfolio as long as possible, there are basically just two primary systems you can utilize. You can concentrate on long haul development and purchase the stocks that ought to acknowledge in an incentive after some time, or you can look for increasingly ordinary returns and purchase stocks that should offer standard profit pay-outs.

Regardless of whether you are effectively exchanging stocks, there are certain impediments included. In exceptionally fundamental terms, you can either purchase stocks that you think will go up in worth or short sell stocks that you think will go down in esteem. There's absolutely a more enormous scope of systems that can be utilized when adopting the purchase and hold strategy, notwithstanding, the adaptability and flexibility in alternatives exchanging implies that you will discover many, a lot more open doors for making benefits in any prevailing economic situation.

For instance, you may have a specific ability for anticipating changes in the forex (foreign trade) showcase just as a robust crucial information on a particular industry. You could utilize your expertise in the forex market to exchange alternatives dependent on remote monetary standards and furthermore utilize your industry information to exchange choices dependent on significant stocks. The potential for finding appropriate exchanges is practically boundless.

Disservices of Option Trading

It's genuinely simple to perceive any reason why exchanging choices are getting progressively well known among numerous financial specialists. It's not, at this point only the experts that are included, in light of the fact that an ever-increasing number of easygoing financial specialists and home brokers are exploiting the advantages on offer. It isn't without its detriments, however.

Most would agree that acing choices exchanging is no essential undertaking, and there is unquestionably a long way to go. This is undoubtedly the single primary motivation why it's despite everything kept away from by such a significant number of, as the complexities of the subject can appear to be overpowering or in any event, threatening. It's absolutely a significant drawback that it's only not as clear the same number of different types of speculation.

Another hindrance is the dangers in question. While there are hazards in any type of venture, exchanging choices can be especially dangerous, particularly for relative tenderfoots who don't have a colossal measure of understanding. Dangers involved with options trading.

In the first experience with alternatives exchanging we have just given a point by point clarification of what choices are and what exchanging them involves, alongside a diagram of the considerable number of preferences. On the off chance that you are genuinely thinking about this type of exchanging as part, or all, of your venture methodology, at that point, these essential subjects are imperative to know.

With any type of contributing, your capital is at last in danger somewhat when you contribute it, and alternatives exchanging is the same. While there are various ways how you can restrict your hazard, through utilizing the suitable exchanging procedures, for instance, there are certain immediate and roundabout dangers that you should know about. On this page, we give further subtleties on this, covering the accompanying:

- Complexities
- Liquidity
- Expenses
- Time Decay

1. Complexities of Options Trading

The very idea of choices exchanging and the complexities included is a hazard in itself. While it isn't generally that hard to comprehend the nuts and bolts, a few parts of alternatives exchanging and the techniques you can utilize are significantly increasingly convoluted. It's a genuinely regular mix-up for financial specialists, and especially fledglings, to not completely comprehend what they are doing, and this can be a very risky slip-up to make.

You can beat this hazard by learning, however much as could be expected, including the propelled subjects and just utilizing techniques that you are totally acquainted with. It's effortless to re-think what you are doing and why, and this is something you should attempt to stay away from. The Information will give you certainty.

2. Liquidity of Options

Choices exchanging is unmistakably more typical than it used to be, with an expanding number of speculators getting included, however, there can even now be a few issues with the liquidity of specific alternatives. Since there are such vast numbers of various sorts, it's very conceivable that a specific choice you wish to exchange may just be exchanged low volume.

This can introduce an issue since it might make it hard to make the necessary exchanges at the correct costs. Is anything but a significant issue on the off chance that you are exchanging minimal volumes or just exchanging the most well-known choices, yet for those exchanging huge volumes or less standard choices, it can make an extra hazard. The trades usually use advertise creators to guarantee certain degrees of liquidity, however, this doesn't really expel the issue.

3. Expenses of Trading Options

Firmly connected to the liquidity of specific alternatives are the costs engaged with exchanging them. The cost of a choices contract is continually cited on the trades with an offer cost and an ask cost. The offer cost is the value you get for thinking of them, and the ask cost is the value you pay for getting them.

The ask cost is consistently higher than the offered cost, and the contrast between these two costs is known as the offer ask spread or the spread. The spread is fundamentally a roundabout expense of exchanging choices, and the higher the spread, the more those costs increment. An absence of liquidity will, for the most part, lead to higher spreads, and this is another possibly critical hazard.

The immediate expenses of exchanging choices can likewise be higher than some different types of speculation: explicitly, the commissions charged by representatives.

Making alternatives spread includes entering at least two situations on various choices that depend on the equivalent fundamental security. There are excellent purposes behind making these spreads, yet the truth of the matter is that taking different positions adequately on a single exchange results in higher commissions.

4. Time Decay

Another unavoidable hazard is the impact of time rot. All alternatives have a period esteem calculated in to them, and ordinarily, the more they have until termination, the higher that time esteem is. Accordingly, any alternatives that you own will consistently be losing a portion of their incentive over the long haul. Obviously, this doesn't imply that they generally go down in esteem, yet time rot can contrarily affect the estimation of any choices that you clutch.

There are a few financial specialists that know about the dangers associated with exchanging alternatives, and as a result of this, they choose to keep away from choices as venture vehicle. The straightforward certainty is that it isn't for everybody; it's a generally unusual approach to contribute, and there are sure entanglements and drawbacks.

In the event that you do feel that exchanging choices is for you, at that point, the following thing you coherently need to know is the place you can purchase, sell, and compose alternatives.

CHAPTER - 21

EXOTIC OPTIONS

An exotic option is one that has a basic structure that differs from either European or American options when it comes to the how and when of how the payout will be provided or how the option relates to the underlying asset in question. Additionally, the number of potential underlying assets is going to be much more varied and can include things like what the weather is like or how much rainfall a given area has experienced. Due to the customization options and the complexity of exotic options, they are only traded over the counter.

While they are undoubtedly more complex to get involved with, exotic options also offer up several additional advantages when compared to common options, including:

They are a better choice for those with particular

needs when it comes to risk management.

They offer up a variety of unique risk dimensions when it comes to both management and trading.

They offer a far more extensive range of potential investments that can more easily meet a diverse number of portfolio's needs.

They are often cheaper than traditional options.

They also have additional drawbacks, the biggest of which is that they often cannot be priced correctly using standard pricing formulas. This may work as a benefit instead of a drawback, however, depending on if the mispricing falls, in favor of the trader or the writer. It is also essential to keep in mind that the amount of risk that is taken on with exotic options is always going to be higher than with other options due to the limited liquidity each type of exotic option is going to have available. While some types are going to have markets that are relatively active, others are only going to have limited interest. Some are even what is known as dual-party transactions, which mean they have no underlying liquidity and are only traded when two amiable traders can be found.

There are many different types of exotic options, including:

Choose option: The most common exotic option

is known as the choose option which allows the investor in question to choose if the option is either a call or a put at different points in the option's lifetime. As this option has the ability to change during the holding period, it is not listed on any regular exchange.

Barrier option: A barrier option is an option type whose payout is going to vary depending on whether the underlying asset has reached a specific price. A barrier option may also be a knock-out at the same time, which means it will expire at $0 if the underlying asset goes over a specific price as well. This then cuts into the profits of the holder but protects the assets of the writer quite nicely. On the contrary, it could also be what is known as a knock-in, which means it will not have any value until the underlying asset reaches a specific price point.

Barrier options are thought of as an exotic option due to their complexity. They also come with the classification because they are a path-dependent option, and their value is based on the value changes of the underlying asset during its terms of existence. Essentially, this means the payoff from this type of option is based on the price path of the asset in question, not necessarily its actual price.

Asian option: An Asian option is an option that pays out based on the underlying assets average price over a set period of time as opposed to when it reaches maturity. This type of option is attractive to some traders as it can help to protect them from a period of high market volatility. It is considered an exotic option because it costs less than the standard American option.

Digital option: A digital option is a type of option with a fixed payout that will payout if the underlying stock reaches or exceeds a specific strike price. A digital option is like a binary option except that it only applies to options based on stocks specifically. If the proposition upon which it is created comes to pass, then the option will be automatically exercised. They are also different from traditional binary options because they are often traded on unregulated platforms. This means that they also carry a higher overall chance of getting caught up in fraudulent activities.

Compound options: A compound option is a type of option that is created with another option as its underlying asset. This means it contains 2 different strike prices along with 2 different exercise dates. There are 4 types of compound options:

- Put on a call

- Call on a put

- Put on a put
- Call on a call

This type of option typically only appears in the fixed income or currency market, where uncertainties regarding a given option's capabilities for risk protection are more prevalent. The advantages of using a compound option include large amounts of leverage at a reduced price. It is essential to keep in mind that the resulting premium will still cost more than a traditional option.

Bermuda options: Bermuda options get their name from the fact that Bermuda is roughly halfway between Europe and the US. Bermuda options can be exercised at the point they expire in addition to other specific times prior to its expiration date. This type of option is useful as it provides the writer with additional control as to when the option could be exercised while also providing the buyer an alternative that costs less than the standard American option without any of the European option restrictions.

Quantity-Adjusting Options: Also known as Quanto options, quantity adjusting options give a buyer access to foreign assets while still allowing them to purchase the option in their own primary currency. This option is an excellent choice for investors who are looking for ways to gain exposure to a new market, but do not want to deal with exchange rate issues to be able to do so.

As an example, if a French investor is looking at Brazilian options due to a favorable economic situation, then they may invest in the BOVESPA Index, which is Brazil's primary stock exchange. To do so without worrying about the exchange rate between the euro and the Brazilian real, they would purchase a quantity adjusting call option for the BOVESPA but denominated using euros. This lets the investor attempt to make their money as they would without worrying about getting a payout that may decrease due to unfavorable exchange rates.

Because it is essentially a two-in-one package, this option will naturally require a more significant premium than average. This fact provides writers of quantity-adjusting options with additional premiums in addition to the additional risk they take on when dealing with exchange rates, so the buyers do not have to.

Look-back options: Look-back options do not have a fixed price from which they can be exercised when they are first created. Instead, the holder of these types of options is free to choose the most favorable price to exercise at any point before the option expires. These options remove all the risk associated with correctly timing the entry to the market, which makes them more expensive than traditional option types.

As an example, assume an investor buys into a call option with the exotic modifier of a 1-month look-back. The exercise price will then be decided once the option matures by taking the lowest price that the underlying stock ended up reaching in its lifetime. The underlying stock ends up at $106 at its expiration time, and the lowest price it achieved was $71, which means the payoff is the difference between $106 and $71 or $35.

Basket option: A basket option is very similar to a vanilla option, with the exception being that they are based on more than a single underlying stock. As an example, if an option pays out based on the price of not just 1 but 3 underlying stocks, then it is considered a basket option. Each underlying asset can then be worth the same amount in the end total, or they can be weighted in various other quantities as well.

CHAPTER - 22

KEYS TO SUCCESS

I want to share with you the keys to success as they relate to probability-based trading. When I'm conducting webinars and seminars, I typically have a slide in the presentation that promises the best, most foolproof indicators on the planet. As the attendees wait impatiently for the answer, I roll to the next slide in the presentation. To their surprise, there is a single slide with the word... SIZE. Then I hear a giant collective groan from the audience.

The truth is size kills. I've experienced that firsthand, and I don't want that to happen to you. The devastating losses I took in October 2008 were strictly because I now thought I knew something. I was trading high probability credit spreads, and they worked great for 15 months. With such great success, I presumed

I had a methodology that worked flawlessly. Month after month, I saw my account grow. As I became more and more comfortable, I kept growing the number of trades. What could go wrong? I have been doing this successfully for over a year with zero drawdowns. Enter October 2008. The sharp down move resulted in devastating losses. If I don't convey any other knowledge to you in this book, I want to encourage you to be very cognizant of your trade size and money management.

The first sign that trade size is too large to me is when a trader/investor is uncomfortable after a trade has gone against them, and panic sets in. When trading the probability-based trading methodology, you accept the risk at entry. Take a moment to process that.

Remember, we accept the risk at the entry. Be comfortable with that risk, and allow the probabilities to work for you.

Just follow the probability-based criteria and allow the math to work

Ideally, we want to place short premium trades when the implied volatility is high relative to the stock or ETF we are trading. We use the metric, Implied Volatility Rank (IVR), to determine if implied volatility is expanded beyond the mean for the stock or ETF we are considering for a trade. IVR compares the current implied volatility of the stock or ETF to where the implied volatility of this stock or ETF has been over the last twelve months.

We use 45 days to expiration as our target for when to place trades. Obviously, 45 days to expiration only occurs once each option cycle. But we place trades throughout the option cycle until there are about 28 days left in the cycle. But 45 days to expiration is the "sweet spot."

This is precisely the essence of what probability-based traders do. They put the odds in their favor by using the criteria correctly and then execute enough trades to allow the math to work.

Once again, back to the coin flip analogy. The more occurrences (trades) that meet the criteria, the closer the results will be to expectations. You allow the odds to work as they should by keeping your trade size small and executing many trades. You're far better trading 10 trades of one lot each then one trade of a 10 lot.

It's Murphy's law. We always think we know what will happen. And with Murphy's law, obviously, the opposite happens.

But for now, I want to share with you, I typically manage winners between 25% to 50% of the premium received.

My typical target is 50% of the premium received. For example, if I'm doing a credit spread and I sell the credit spread, and I collect a dollar in premium, I'm typically looking to buy that back for 50 cents. That will give you an idea of what I mean by managing your winners.

Managing winners is in strict contrast to what the "self-proclaimed" experts profess. Weren't we always taught to "manage losers and let the winners run?" Probability-based trading has proven this is not the way to consistency.

Trades are managed mechanically and non-emotionally when there are 21 days left in the expiration cycle. At this benchmark, we have 3 choices for trade management. Assuming the profit target is not reached by this benchmark, this is the mechanical management process:

Exit the trade for any profit or scratch

If the trade cannot be exited for any profit or scratched, roll the trade to a farther out expiration provided if the roll is for a credit or zero. We do not add capital to the trade.

If the trade cannot be managed according to either of the above steps, we remain in the trade. Remember, we accepted the risk at entry, and we let the trade play-out for the remaining 21 days in the cycle.

Don't follow the advice from the "experts." They maintain "manage your losers, let the winners run." Probability-based trading proves this is not the roadmap to consistency.

Remember, duration always trumps direction. We may have a directional bias when we trade, but we aren't directional traders.

It is worth repeating to quit obsessing with "being right." Allow our expertise and not our egos to drive our trading. Probability-based training is not about being right. Probability-based trading is finding opportunities that meet your criteria, executing those trades, and mechanically managing the trades.

You understand the markets have an upward bias. There is about a 53 to 47 upward bias

Implied volatility is more significant than actual volatility, the preponderance of the time. And that's how we make our living with probability-based trading. We sell premium when the volatility is beyond its mean. We are receiving more premium and expecting a reversion to the mean.

Implied volatility is usually mean reverting. As stated in point #2, we want to sell volatility when it has expanded. This is because we have every reason to believe it will revert to the mean. It might not always revert to the mean in the cycle we're trading. But you can rest assured that volatility reverts to the mean.

These 3 facts are essential to know and understand. They represent keys to success with probability-based trading.

CHAPTER - 23

SELECTING A GOOD BROKER

Many times in this text, a reference was made to professional advice and guidance before and during any trading with options. In a few cases, it was also suggested that this advice and guidance, was to be rendered by experts and not just professionals. But who are these people?

They are called options brokers, and their profession is to offer actual options trading, along with research, education and various tools to individual investors. Apart from the above, they can also offer trade in other financial products related to options, like stocks, funds (either mutual or exchange-traded) and bonds.

As in any profession, there are good brokers and brokers that do not have your best interest in their minds. Here are the things to look for in order to select a good options broker.

First of all, you need to know if you want to deal with a regular broker or a reseller broker. The first one deals directly with you, while the latter intermediates between you and a larger broker.

Regular brokers have a better reputation than resellers, especially those that are members of recognized organizations like F.IN.R.A. (Financial Industry Regulatory Authority) or S.I.P.C. (Securities Investor Protection Corporation). Therefore, if you choose a regular broker, the first thing to check is whether they belong to such an entity. If not, it would be best to avoid them.

The next choice to make is between a full service broker and a discount broker. The full service ones offer a lot more services, but they do not come cheap. They undertake the more significant part of the work to be done, and they will offer the professional advice and guidance required.

On the other hand, a discount broker may be the best choice for a beginner. For two reasons:

a) The fees of a full service one are probably not affordable for a newcomer and

b) You will learn a lot more about options trading if you do what is required yourself

Regardless of the above, what usually affects the decisions on which broker to choose, are the costs involved. The following will weigh a lot on your selection:

1) Minimum balances

In order to start a brokerage account, most brokers require a minimum balance. This amount ranges between $500 and $1,000.

2) Margin accounts

While it is not an immediate choice for beginners, it will be a significant issue as you continue trading. Margin accounts are created when the broker will lend you the money to make the trades. The securities and options that you will trade, along with the balance of your account, are held as collateral.

While it is risky (you stand to file for bankruptcy if you fail grossly), it is a handy tool with which to check the integrity of your broker. A good broker will protest, if your choices are not sound ones, and will not lend you the money as they do not want to lose it.

3) Easiness of withdrawal

Just like any other professionals, brokers want to make a profit. Therefore, most of them will charge you a withdrawal fee, or will not let you close your account if the balance drops below the minimum. It is strongly recommended to make sure that you fully understand the rules in reference to money withdrawal before you begin any cooperation with a broker.

4) Fee structures

Hidden fees and expenses are the greatest fear of investors. While most brokers follow similar rules, there are some of them who have particularly complex fee structures. A general rule of thumb is that if the fees look too good to be true, make sure that you read the small print. Generally, the less complicated the fee structure is, the better the broker.

Brokers are significant, as you will not be able to start investing without a brokerage account. You should always keep in mind that no broker can be good at everything. So the last issue to consider before selecting a broker is what kind of investor you are. Your broker must match with your style.

CHAPTER - 24

OPTIONS PRICING MODELS

You just have to understand a few good models DEEPLY, and then use a calculator online.

The Black-Scholes Model

In 1973, Robert Merton, Myron Scholes, and Fischer Black introduced the Black-Scholes pricing model as a way of computing option premium. Since then, this model has become the most popular. In fact, Merton and Scholes received a Nobel Prize in Economics two years after Black died in 1995. Black, however, was still acknowledged for his role, although he wasn't given the Nobel Prize because the Nobel is awarded to living persons only.

The Black-Scholes model is applicable only to European options, both call and put, and doesn't include paid dividends in its calculation. However, it can still be used by using the ex-dividend value of the asset.

The model assumes that the option can only be exercised at the time it expires. And that's why only European options are considered. Furthermore, aside from not considering paid dividends, this model also doesn't take into consideration any commissions.

It also assumes that the market is efficient and that the movements in the market aren't predictable. Volatility and risk-free interest rates are constant and known. Lastly, the Black-Scholes model assumes that returns are distributed normally.

This option only takes into consideration one risky asset, such as a stock, and then a risk-free asset, such as cash. With this, there is no arbitrage opportunity, but there is a way for someone to borrow money at a risk-free rate with this model. You can also buy any stock with this model, even a fraction of it, without any hidden fees or costs. With this option, the derivatives are determined at the current moment, and the payoff as well. You can create a great stock investment with a low option investment.

To compute for the option value, the Black-Scholes model requires the following:

- Risk-free interest rate

- Implied volatility

- Timing (expressed as a percentage of the year)

- Strike price

- The current price of the underlying asset

The mathematical formula is complicated. An average person may be intimidated to use it. Fortunately, there are options calculators available online which can be used to compute for the price using this model. Furthermore, there are analysis tools provided by trading platforms which be used to compute for the price.

This is an excellent way to get an approximation of the investment, but it's not the only thing you should be relying on. Due to the volatility of the market, liquidity risks, and sudden changes and risks, it could cause you to expose yourself to some significant risks. There are also extreme price changes, and most of the time, money does not come with an unchanging value in the real world. It's an excellent way to get a feel for what you're about to do, but at the same time, you shouldn't rely entirely on this.

The Cox-Rubinstein Binomial Option Pricing Model

A variation of the Black-Scholes model, the Cox-Ross-Rubenstein model, was developed by

Mark Edward Rubenstein, Stephen Ross, and Carrington Cox. The primary advantage of this model is that it uses a lattice-based model and takes into consideration the price movement of the underlying asset over time. A lattice-based model considers the changes in different variables over the life of the option. Therefore, it results to a more accurate option price. It looks similar to a tree, and it progresses in that manner to the expiration of the stock.

This model is used for American options. It assumes that everyone is indifferent to risk, so the returns are equivalent to the risk-free interest rate.

The Cox-Ross-Rubenstein model further assumes that arbitrage isn't possible because the market is perfectly efficient. The price of the underlying asset can never go up and down simultaneously. It can only go in one direction at any given time. Different points in time can be specified during the life of the option. Because of this, it is possible to create a binomial tree.

Typically, it's calculated from the beginning of the option to the end of it, and then back again. Once that's done, it's then calculated with the factors of the changes in dividend prices, along with the changes in option prices. All of this is calculated together and put into a theoretical model to help others understand where their money will be going.

The most significant advantage of this is that it works for American stocks. Another benefit is that it also helps you see exactly where a stock is at a specific point. You can take a look at this, and through the analytic properties of it, you'll know where that stock will be approximately in the future. It's helpful in that regard.

The most significant limitation, however, is that it takes forever to calculate. You're examining a ton of numbers all at the same time, and many of the older computers can't do it. With the changes in technology, however, the software is able to keep up with the speed of changing numbers. It's advisable that you get an online calculator in order to see where a stock will be at a certain point in time.

Like the Cox-Ross-Rubenstein model, online pricing calculators and analysis tools provided by trading platforms can be used to know the option price.

The Put/Call Parity

As a pricing concept, the put/call parity was introduced by Hans Stoll in 1969. According to his study, there is a relationship between the European call and put options with similar strike price and expiration date.

It means that for every call option value at a particular strike price, there's a corresponding put option value for it. The same goes for put option values. There's a corresponding call option value for a put option value at a specific strike price. The relationship exists because a position is created, which is the same position as the underlying asset when there's a combination of put and call options.

The returns must be similar for the underlying asset and option so that arbitrage won't arise. Traders and investors who take advantage of arbitrage can make a profit if the opportunity arises.

The put/call parity is used to test pricing models for European options. If the result of the pricing model doesn't satisfy the parity check, it means that arbitrage can occur, and the model must be rejected as a pricing strategy. There are several ways to compute for the put/call parity.

Luckily, some trading platforms offer analysis tools. These provide visualizations of the put/call parity.

But of course, you don't have to memorize all the pricing models thoroughly. Just pick one suitable for your situation, have an online pricing model calculator handy, and let the numbers move for you.

CHAPTER - 25

DEVELOP A TRADING PLAN

Develop a Trading Plan

A trading plan acts as a guide during your trading process. It is crucial to have one, especially if you want to earn huge profits from trading options. Below are some of the points to consider while making a trading plan:

1. Set Goals

If you want to succeed at something, you need to come up with a goal, target or ambition that inspires you to work hard and accomplish what you are doing. As a beginner in the option trading industry, what change would you like to see in your life? Why would you like to trade options? Well, I'm sure that most people join this industry with the expectations of earning a fortune out of trading options.

Write down every goal that you have in mind and allow the goals to be a source of inspiration anytime you want to trade options. This ensures that you do not give up or lose hope in the process. You keep trading with the hope that things will get better, and you will achieve the dreams that you have.

Goals can be powerful tools that connect us to our future success.

2. Know How You Can Handle Success

Eventually, when you become an expert trader, you are likely to earn high profits. How you utilize the income generated determines if you will keep earning more or you remain stagnant at one point. As a wise investor, you need to use your finances properly. You can utilize them well for the sake of the future success.

This can involve reinvesting the income earned. By reinvesting, you keep earning more and more with each passing day. The good thing about option trading is that your earnings are not limited. You can trade as many times as you wish in a single day and earn big profits daily. When you master that art of trading options, it gets more comfortable with each day. You get to make huge profits effortlessly. However, while reinvesting, avoid using all the accumulated income.

Overconfidence can cause you to start making losses in options trading.

3. Know How to Handle Failure

Like any other investment, one is bound to incur a loss or a profit. Profits are excellent, but losses are terrible nightmares. As a beginner, it is advisable that one takes up what one can handle.

If you are new to the option trading industry, avoid investing money that you cannot afford to lose. In an event, the trade goes contrary to what you anticipated; you will end up incurring huge losses. Each day we are having thousands of people joining options trading with high expectations. Some believe that it's an easy short cut or way to get rich faster. Contrary to their belief, they have to put in a lot of effort to ensure that they can start earning from trading options.

Most of these diseases are caused by factors that we create on our own. An individual might be suffering from depression after making a big loss while trading options. This can be avoided by being prepared in case things do not move as expected.

4. Access Your Market Knowledge

Most people start trading options with very little knowledge of what it entails. As a result, they end up incurring huge losses since they lacked the required information. It's a good thing that you are already reading this book since it shows that you realize the importance of having information. Chances are, you will be highly equipped, unlike most people. The interesting fact about trading options is that there is something new to be learned on a daily basis. As the market expands and grows, more and more things are being discovered.

This allows you to know the best time to trade and also avoid trading when the market is not favorable. At the same time, you acquire some tips and tactics that enhance your trading skill, making you better than you were while beginning.

All the information is available on the internet and in books that you can easily access.

5. Know the Options Strategies

Option strategies form the basis of option trading. It goes with doubt that if you aspire to be an expert in option trading, you need to be aware of all the option strategies that you can utilize in a particular trade. Depending on the circumstances and factors surrounding a trade, different strategies will work in different situations. Some people are only aware of a few option strategies that they use in almost all the trades that they engage in. As a result, they end up making big losses, since the option strategies they used were not best suited for that trade.

This is a mistake most beginners make. In as much as you may be comfortable using a particular option strategy, you need to be fully aware of your other options. Ensure that you increase your knowledge for you to stand a better chance of succeeding at what you do. Once you are aware of all the strategies that you can utilize, you can easily make a trading plan. It allows you to know when to trade, when to hold and when not to trade at all.

6. Plan Your Entry and Exist

For one to be an expert in trading, they need to have a proper plan on when to exit and enter a trade. Some brokerage accounts provide graphs and analyses for the current option market. By analyzing the graphs, there is a lot of information that you can pick up. You get to evaluate the graph movements and look for signals that encourage you to enter a trade. Often, you get in a trade when the conditions around it are favorable, and the probability of succeeding in that particular trade is high.

When the conditions are not favorable or welcoming, it acts as a signal to avoid that particular trade so that you do not end up making a loss. Most people are good when it comes to the entry of a particular trade. Unfortunately, most do not know when to exit. As a result, they end up incurring losses, since they missed the exit signals.

The same way you analyze the graph to know the best time to enter a trade. Is the same way you should analyze it to know the best time to exit a trade.

This will save you from incurring losses.

7. Analyze Your Trading Progress

The best way to trace your trading progress is by writing down everything that you do. Have a journal where you write down your trading progress.

There are a lot of things that you will note once you start doing this. It allows you to know the best times you had while trading. You get to know the strategies that you utilized at that time, which led to your trading success. It allows you to see the trends and circumstances that resulted in a good and successful trade. All this information is relevant to your growth in the option trading industry. On the other hand, you become aware of the circumstances surrounding the unsuccessful trades that you might have had. It is also good to look at the amount of money you spent at various trades and how you were able to recover it after the trade. On the same note, look at the money that you lost.

Compare your success rates and your loss rates. See if the choices you are making are worth it.

This will help you grow in the option trading industry.

8. Establish Your Risk Tolerance

While trading options, you will come across both risks and rewards. Every trader aspires to get a reward while trading options. After all, the point of investing is to earn profits. No one likes to make a loss. We keep working hard and improving so that we can stand a better chance of succeeding in the option trading industry.

As a beginner or a person who is green in this field, there are a lot of factors that you will have to consider, especially if you want to make a living out of trading. It's not every day that you will be lucky while trading options, you will come across some bad days, where you make losses.

Most people have a bad perception that option trading is a shortcut into getting rich. When you approach it with these perceptions, you will end up being frustrated. Like any other investment, option trading comes with its own risks. As a trader, you need to be aware of these risks and know how you will work your way around it to have a successful outcome.

Know what you can afford to lose so that you can determine what you can risk.

9. Have a Trading Routine

A trader needs to set a time when they can analyze the various trade movements. At times we invest in option trading blindly without analyzing the trade market. When things go contrary to what we expected, we end up concluding that option trading is a scam since we got nothing out of it. Well, the problem is that we do not take time to learn.

Spare some time to analyze your trades and get to see how you managed to succeed and what led to a loss, if at all, there was any. You also get to know the best time to carry out a trade and when to avoid carrying out a trade.

A routine will also help in tracking your progress.

10. Identify What to Trade

The option trading market is wide, and there are numerous trading parameters that you can decide to engage in. You could be a currency trader, stock trader or join the other available trade markets. The decision you make entirely depends on you. However, before making that decision, it is important to equip yourself with all the necessary information regarding option markets.

Analyze the various markets to know what you can engage in and what to avoid engaging in. While studying, you will identify the pro and cons of the various markets. It is entirely up to you to know which market is worth spending your energy and finances. Select a market that you are well conversant with and determine how you will succeed in that particular market. While making this decision, it is important to fully depend on yourself. What may have worked for your friend may not work for you. They may have chosen a market that they are well aware of, and if you make a mistake of choosing the same, you may end up making losses.

This process is very crucial and essential while trading options.

CHAPTER - 26

3 SELLING OPTIONS

If you have 100 or more shares of a particular stock, you can sell covered calls against your shares. This is a common strategy used by people to earn money off their shares, but you always face the risk that your shares will be called away if the option is exercised. One strategy that can be used is to sell out of the money calls when you don't expect the share price to rise to the strike price of the call option over the lifetime of the contract.

For example, Facebook is trading at $190.25 a share. You can sell a $210 call for $0.64, so for all 100 shares, one option contract would net you $64. This is for an expiration date in 30 days. Or you could take a higher level of risk and sell a $195 call for $4.05, which would give you a premium of $405 per option contract. If you had 500 shares, then you'd receive $2,025 in premiums. Not a bad passive income, and all you have to do is hope that the share price stays below the strike price.

If the share price closes in on the strike price, then you will be faced with a dilemma – risk having the option exercised if the share price rises above the strike price or you can buy back the option and cut into your profits. With a few days left to expiration, the option you sold may be worth $2.05, so you could buy back the five options you sold, and you'd reduce your net profit to $1,000.

You could go further out, even selling LEAPS. In that case, the premium paid is much larger. A Facebook LEAP with a $195 call that expires in 18 months has a premium of $30.58, so selling five contracts for your 500 shares could bring in an income of $15,290. Of course, there is a higher risk that the share price will rise above the strike price over an 18-month period than there is over the short term.

The one principle to keep in mind selling covered calls is that you could lose your shares if the option is exercised. With that in mind, you should only select a strike price that is of a higher amount than what you had paid for the shares. That way if you are forced to sell the shares, then you are not taking a loss doing so. That can make losing the shares easier to deal with. So if we had purchased our shares at $200 a share, we would not select a $195 strike price because that represents a potential loss, which would be given by the price we paid for the shares minus the strike price and then less the premium aid, in this case, $200 - $195 - $4.05 so we'd end up losing $0.95 on the trade. If you had purchased the shares at a lower price, say $190 a share, then the $195 strike would make sense since if the stock price rose and the shares were called away, we'd still profit by selling the shares.

Protected puts are the put version of a covered call. The risk with a protected put is that the shares will be "put to you," and you will have to buy the shares, so you will be required to have enough capital in your account in order to cover the purchase.

Of course, the trick to selling options is to pick a strike price where you think the option will expire worthlessly. There is always the risk that you are wrong, but if you think the share price is going to rise for Facebook, to use an example, you could sell a protected $190 put for $4.95, earning $495 per contract. If the share price rises, the options would expire worthlessly, and you would keep the premium and profit from the deal.

Selling Naked Puts

Selling naked puts is a popular strategy for traders that are given level 4 status. If you can get this level from your broker, you can consider this possibly profitable strategy. Of course, the key is choosing the right strike price.

When a put is "naked," that means it isn't backed by anything. However, you are still required by law to fulfill your obligations should the option be exercised, but one way that traders avoid this problem is by buying the options back if there is a chance they would be exercised. Time value may work in your favor, which will make the options cheaper and so you can buy them back and still profit.

Another consideration is to choose a relatively low implied volatility, which reduces the chances that the stock will move much over the lifetime of the option. But that is a trade-off as well, as implied volatility that is a few points higher can result in a large increase in the premium received for selling the option.

Consider IBM. The stock price is at $139.20, but you could sell a 30 day $135 put for $2.44, or $244. You could even sell in the money puts. A $145 put would sell for $748 if you sold five contracts that would be a 30-day income of $3,640.

Selling in the money puts could be risky, but beneficial if it was believed that IBM shares were set to rise in price. If the price rises above the strike price, then the options will expire worthlessly.

Selling LEAPS, while it carries higher risk since a long time to expiration, gives a higher probability that the option will move in the amount, also allow you to sell at high premiums. A $130 put for IBM expiring in 18 months would sell for $13.20, so selling five contracts would give you a premium of $6,600. Bid-Ask spreads can be large for LEAPS, and the volume is probably small. For this particular option, we find that the bid-ask spread is about 80 cents, which isn't too bad, meaning selling it might not be that difficult. Daily volume is small at 10, but the open interest is 1,282. Experienced traders often recommend an open interest of 500 or higher since that indicates there are enough people buying the contracts.

The risk with naked puts is that you will be forced to buy the shares. Again, if it looks like that might turn out to be the case, you can buy the contracts back. Selling out of the money options that expire in the near term can leave you in a better position since the options will probably expire worthlessly, and you will be able to keep the premium without having to buy back the options. If you have to buy the shares, the loss would be the share price minus the market price. But of course, you'd have to get the capital to buy the shares as well.

So if you sold a put option on IBM with a strike price of $138 expiring in 6 weeks, it would sell for $3.70. If the share price dropped to $136, you'd have to use cash to buy the shares at $138, and possibly lose $2 a share by selling them – or you could simply keep them and wait for the price to go back up. Plus, your loss would be offset by the premium, so your break-even point is the amount of the strike price minus the premium paid.

Selling Naked Calls

You can also sell naked calls. This means that you sell call options without owning the shares of stock. The risk that the option will be exercised means that you would have to buy the shares at a higher market price and then sell them at the lower strike price. So the key here would be to sell out of the money calls at strike prices that you doubt the stock will reach over the lifetime of the option. The same strategies can be used, and if it looks like the share price is rising, you can buy the options back to avoid being assigned.

Looking at IBM, some modest out of the money call options 30 days to expiration have good prices. A $141 call, which is almost $2 out of the money is $3.55, so selling one contract would give you $355.

Suppose that a stock was trading at $195 a share. You could sell a call with a 45-day expiration with a strike price of $200 for $4.46, or $446. If we find that the share price has risen to $197 with 10 days to expiration, the calls would now be priced at $1.88, or $188. So you could buy them back and still have a profit of $258 per contract, avoiding the risk that you would be assigned if the share price kept rising. Of course, at $3 out of the money, you might wait. When the price of the share rises to $199 with seven days left, the calls would be $218, so you'd be cutting a little more into your profits. But if it dropped $1 the next day, then the call option would only be worth $1.58.

Remember, when you sell options, you make money on the time premium. Or put another way, time decay is your friend. Out of the money, options lose value rapidly as the expiration date approaches.

The biggest risk with selling naked call options if you can't buy them back is having to buy the shares at a high price and then selling them at a loss to honor your obligations. Supposed that a stock is trading at $95 a share, and you sell a call option that has a $100 strike price. If the stock breaks out and, say, rises to $130 a share, someone might exercise the option. Since you sold the call naked, you'd be forced to buy the shares at $130 and sell them at the $100 strike price, losing $30 a share, which would be partially offset by the premium, which might be around $1 per share.

So selling naked calls can be profitable, but carries a lot of risks as well. The key to selling naked calls successfully is picking the right strike price and choosing a stock that you don't believe is going to be having price movements that are large enough to cause the option to be in the money.

Broker May Force Sale

Note that options that expire in the money may be automatically exercised by most brokerages. So you will not want to let an option expire in the money unless you are prepared to buy or sell the shares as required.

CHAPTER - 27

PREDICTING DIRECTIONS

The world is full of uncertainty, and the stock market responds accordingly. Sure, financial instruments are based on the so-called fundamentals like monetary policy, interest rates, and equity essentials like sales and taxes. We have a stereotype of market makers as being steely-eyed, cold, and calculating automatons. They are not. They are human beings and are as emotionally involved in the market as an investor, 'man-on-the-street,' or anyone else. Emotions often affect the market based on the sometimes irrational response to this uncertainty. Recent events like the BREXIT outcome are examples of that emotional reaction.

The Basic Academic Economic Theory assumes that investors act rationally, i.e., a manner that best satisfies their economic interests. In the real world, markets do not always act rationally because human beings do not always act rationally.

Certain internal events will affect market performance like the end of quarter movements by fund managers to establish positions to make their quarterly reports look better. You can also observe drops in stock prices and indexes on Fridays, as holders get ready for the weekend by taking profits. Predicting market moves is sometimes like reading tea leaves, with a similar amount of hocus-pocus and mystery. However, successful investors learn or develop a sense of where the market is going and when.

There are five things an investor must do to succeed. They are pretty obvious, but we need to keep them in mind. The first is the Fundamental Analysis. The second is the Technical Analysis. They are sort of the 'meat and potatoes' of trading. Perhaps more important are the next three, Intuition, Patience, and Attention.

Intuition

Intuition can lead to many really good investments. Some years ago, a family was making regular vacation trips from Michigan to Florida. They soon noticed a new restaurant chain along the interstate highway called Cracker Barrel. Whenever they stopped at one, they had to stand in line, and the food was very good and at good prices. As they made more trips, they noticed that more and more Cracker Barrel restaurants were opening, all with the same waiting line. They invested in CRBL and watched the stock rise, from their entry price of about $5.00 to today's trading range of $150 to $175. That decision was an excellent example of intuition in trading. CBRL had identified a niche and filled it with good service and products.

L'eggs is a similar story. Consumers quickly reacted positively to the quality of the product and the catchy advertising, introduced in 1969. Those L'eggs plastic egg-like containers were a hit with crafts workers and carried the stock of Hanes to new highs. Many investors noticed that L'eggs was the right product at the time, was good quality, and had an exciting marketing promotion. This is the essence of the Intuition component of successful investing. Look for products that are satisfying a market niche, have good quality, and are well received by consumers.

Patience

Investing in the market, whether by buying and selling stocks themselves or by trading in options, requires patience. Sometimes an investor gets nervous and makes an irrational move just out of uncertainty. Traders must learn to be patient. No market moves so fast that the trader cannot make the proper trade in response to some change. Remember, options trading is not for the faint of heart. Nervous responses to extraneous conditions can wreck a well-planned strategy.

Attention

There is also no substitute for paying attention to the market and your positions. No, you do not have to spend every hour of every day watching the big boards. Remember that trading options are not a 'set it and forget it' activity. Traders can build very solid portfolios and make a handsome profit, but like any other job, the trader has to be current, not just in the market moves but also in global news and reports. Some resources have delightful features like daily free videos on changes in the market and outlooks from their experts. Keeping current is essential. Some traders will close out all positions while they are on vacation, and then resume trading when they return. And since most people use portable computer devices, laptops, tablets, smartphones, and so forth, they can spend time even on vacation, trading, and investing. Either way, you choose to do it, remember that options trading requires the investor to pay attention. Make that commitment before you start.

There are many tools available to traders and analysts to predict what is going to happen, at least to some extent. There are two schools of thought on the subject of market predicting; technical and fundamental methods used by informed investors. Most traders use a mixture of the two.

Fundamental Analysis

Fundamental analysis looks at several indicators to determine, at least as an estimate, of the direction of the economy, various industry groups, and individual stocks.

It begins with the general trend of the entire economy, both national and global. That old saying about the flapping wings of a butterfly in Africa causing a hurricane in Florida suggests that no national economy exists in a vacuum. There is an enormous interaction between them and among them. When the general economy rises, just like the tide, all individual boats rise, but not necessarily equally. Similarly, when the economy contracts, all sectors contract, but not equally. Some sectors will contract more than others. In an expanding economy, sectors like technology, biotech, electronics manufacturing, and cyclical industries like major appliances and automobiles tend to expand.

Here are some more cyclical industries:

- Heavy equipment

- Discretionary consumer goods

- Machines and tooling

- Restaurants and hotels

- Airlines

Typically, these stocks have a high Beta (β), meaning they respond quickly and strongly to fluctuations in the national and global economies.

Non-cyclical industries are those who are relatively safe during downturns, sectors like utilities, consumer staples, energy, and retailers. Counter-cyclical are those that can even thrive in economic downturns, like discount retailers, auto parts retailers, and big-box building suppliers.

Importantly for options traders, option prices respond to the volatility and trend of the underlying stocks, so traders need to pay close attention to the economic cycle and the sectors of interest to them.

When an investor or options trader has identified the economic trend, i.e., expanding, or contracting, she will then focus on a sector of interest like durable goods, finance, or hospitality, to name just a few. Within that sector or industry, she will then examine the individual companies, looking for those who will lead the way. She will do this by evaluating the company's business model, business plan, management quality, and firm financials. Assessments of business models and business plans can be gained from resources like analyst's reports, annual reports, and public commentary. She will examine management quality by looking at results, internal business indicators like return on investment, return on sales, and debt levels compared with market capitalization. She will read and understand the various documents like the balance sheet, the income or profit and loss statement, cash flow positions, and debt positions for the firm she is interested in. Most of this information is available online and through public documents, including annual reports. Documents like annual reports, of course, are written by insiders and may not be completely objective. Various industry analysts and experts may offer more objective insights. These are available through brokers and online sites.

Technical Analysis

Many investors base their trading decisions on technical factors that look at past performance with knowledge of present and past economic conditions. This analysis is dominated by examining charts that reflect stock performance over some time. Using these charts, they can estimate upcoming stock moves and therefore act on those forecasts by buying and selling options. The following charts describe some important market moves that any options trader needs to know.

The Symmetrical Triangle in Chart 1 shows a stock that is trading within a diminishing range. The upper line represents a resistance line, and the lower is the support line. As the price varies between these converging lines, it is often an indication of a coming breakout. With a breakout to the upside, the options trader will buy calls to cover a long position in anticipation of the upside swing. On the other hand, if the pattern shows a likelihood of a breakout below the support line, the trader might choose to buy puts in anticipation of the drop in market price.

Chart 1 Triangle Pattern

Triangle patterns can also be pointed upward or downward, showing a general tendency for the stock to rise or fall.

Chart 2 shows a condition called a triple top. The horizontal dotted line below the chart is the support line, and the upper dotted line is the resistance line. The chart shows the market price breaking out low. This is an occasion to sell puts. The pattern could have broken out upward, crossing the resistance line.

Notice that that chart can also be inverted, making a triple bottom. These charts indicate the direction of the stock and tips the options trader off to trade in either puts or calls.

Chart 2 Triple Top

Chart 3 shows a pattern called 'head and shoulders.' This is slightly different from a triple top pattern in that the middle peak tends to be higher. Head and shoulders patterns can breakout either up or down. Either way, it presents an opportunity for options traders. The dotted line shows the recent support line. This pattern happens to break out down, but it very well could have broken out upward.

Chart 3 Head and Shoulders

Bollinger Bands

Bollinger bands are probability bands around a moving average line. These bands are usually set at either 1 or 2 standard deviations from the historical stock prices, the closing prices for each day. Movement outside the Bollinger Bands indicates a change in the underlying stock reflecting market changes. Breaking through the Bollinger Band acts as a signal to the options trader to take action.

Many other technical indicators are valuable to options traders. The various resources will provide excellent education and insights to both fundamental and technical analysis techniques. Most investors and traders use both fundamental and technical analysis, and the combination is a personal preference. Just make sure you are familiar with the various indicators and what they can tell you. Be careful to use the correct tools for each condition. There is no "one size fits all" tool; each trader has to develop her system of analysis. The key to success is Intuition, Patience, and Attention.

CHAPTER - 28

RISK MANAGEMENT

Excellent risk management can save the worst trading strategy, but horrible risk management will sink even the best strategy. This is a lesson that many traders learn painfully over time, and I suggest you learn this by heart and install it deep within you even if you can't fully comprehend that statement.

Risk management has many different elements to both quantitative and qualitative. When it comes to options trading, the quantitative side is minimal thanks to the nature of options limiting risk by themselves. However, the qualitative side deserves a lot of attention.

Risk

So, what is a risk anyway? Logically, it is the probability of you losing all of your money. In trading terms, you can think of it as being the probability of your actions, putting you on a path to losing all of your capital. An excellent way to think about the need for proper risk management is to ask yourself what a lousy trader would do? Forget trading, what would a lousy business person do with their capital?

Well, they would spend it on useless stuff that adds nothing to the bottom line. They would also increase expenses, market poorly, not take care of their employees, and be undisciplined with regards to their processes. While trading, you don't have employees or marketing needs, so you don't need to worry about that.

Do you have suppliers and costs? Well, yes, you do. Your supplier is your broker, and you pay fees to execute your trades. That is the cost of access. In directional trading, you have high costs as well because taking losses is a necessary part of trading. With market neutral or non-directional trading, your losses are going to be minimal, but you should still seek to minimize them.

What about discipline? Do you think you can trade and analyze the market thoroughly if you've just returned home from your job and are tired? If you didn't sleep properly last night? Or if you've argued with your spouse or partner? The point I'm making is that the more you behave like a terrible business owner, the more you increase your risk of failure.

Odds and Averages

Trading requires you to think a bit differently about profitability. I spoke about minimizing costs, and your first thought must have been to seek to reduce losses and maximize wins. This is a natural product of linear or ordered thinking. The market, however, is chaotic, and linear thinking is going to get you nowhere.

Instead, you need to think in terms of averages and odds. Averages imply that you need to worry about your average loss size and your average win size. Seek to decrease the former and increase the latter. Notice that when we talk about averages, we're not necessarily talking about reducing the total number of losses. You can reduce the average by either reducing the sum of your losses or by increasing the number of losing trades while keeping the sum of the losses constant. This is a shift in thinking you must make.

Thinking in this way sets you up nicely to think in terms of odds because, in chaotic systems, all you can bank on are odds playing out in the long run. For example, if you flip a coin, do you know in advance whether it's going to be heads or tails? Probably not. But if someone asked you to predict the distribution of heads versus tails over 10,000 flips, you could reasonably guess that it'll be 5000 heads and 5000 tails. You might be off by a few flips either way, but you'll be pretty close percentage-wise.

The greater the number of flips, the lesser your error percentage. This is because the odds inherent in a pattern that occurs in a chaotic system express themselves best over the long run. Your trading strategy is precisely such a pattern. The market is a chaotic system. Hence, you should focus on executing your strategy as it is meant to be executed over and over again and worry about profitability only in the long run.

Contrast this with the usual attitude of traders who seek to win every single trade. This is impossible to accomplish since no trading strategy or pattern is correct 100% of the time.

This is because you do not have to do much when trading options. You enter and then monitor the trade. Sure, it helps to have some directional bias, but even if you get it wrong, your losses will be extremely limited, and you're more likely to hit winners than losers.

Despite this, always think of your strategy in terms of its odds. There are two basic metrics to measure this. The first is the win rate of your system. This is simply the percentage of winners you have. The second is your payout ratio, which is the average win size divided by the average loss size.

Together, these two metrics will determine how profitable your system is. Both of them play off one another, and an increase in one is usually met by a decrease in another. It takes an extremely skillful trader to increase both simultaneously.

Risk per Trade

The quantitative side of risk management when it comes to options trading is lesser than what you need to take care of when trading directionally. However, this doesn't mean there's nothing to worry about. Perhaps the most important metric of them all is your risk per trade. The risk per trade is what ultimately governs your profitability.

How much should you risk per trade? Common wisdom says that you should restrict this to 2% of your capital. For options trading purposes, this is perfectly fine. Once you build your skill and can see opportunities better, I'd suggest increasing it to a higher level.

A point that you must understand here is that you must keep your risk per trade consistent for it to have any effect. You might see a wonderful setup and think that it has no chance of failure, but the truth is that you don't know how things will turn out. Even the prettiest setup has every chance of failing, and the ugliest setup you can think of may result in a profit. So never adjust your position size based on how something looks.

Calculating your position size for a trade is a pretty straightforward task. Every option's strategy will have a fixed maximum risk amount. Divide the capital risk by this amount, and that gives you your position size. Round that down to the nearest whole number since you can only buy whole number lots when it comes to contract sizes.

For example, let's say your maximum risk is $50 per lot on the trade. Your capital is $10,000. Your risk per trade is 2%. So, the amount you're risking on that trade is 2% of 10,000, which is $200. Divide this by 50, and you get 4. Hence, your position size is four contracts or 400 shares. (You'll buy the contracts, not the shares.)

Why is it important to keep your risk per trade consistent? Well, recall that your average win and loss size is important when it comes to determining your profitability. These, in conjunction with your strategy's success rate, determine how much money you'll make. If you keep shifting your risk amount per trade, you'll shift your win and loss sizes. You might argue that since it's an average, you can always adjust amounts to reflect an average.

My counter to that is, how would you know which trades to adjust in advance? You won't know which ones are going to be a win or a loss, so you won't know which trade sizes to adjust to meet the average. Hence, keep it consistent across all trades and let the math work for you.

Aside from risk per trade, there are some simple metrics you should keep track of as part of your quantitative risk management plan.

Drawdown

A drawdown refers to the reduction in capital your account experiences. Drawdowns by themselves always occur. The metrics you should be measuring are the maximum drawdown and recovery period. If you think of your account's balance as a curve, the maximum drawdown is the biggest peak to trough distance in dollars. The recovery period is the subsequent time it took for your account to make new equity high.

If your risk per trade is far too high, your max drawdown will be unacceptably high. For example, if you risk 10% per trade and lose two in a row, which is very likely, your drawdown is going to be 20%. This is an absurdly large hole to dig your way out. Consider that your capital has decreased by 20%, and the subsequent climb back up needs to be done on lesser capital

This is why you need to keep your risk per trade

low and in line with your strategy's success rate. The best way to manage drawdowns and limit the damage they cause is to put in place risk limits per day, week, and month. Even professional athletes who train to do one thing all the time have bad days, so it's unfair to expect yourself to be at 100% all the time.

These risk limits will take you out of the game when you're playing poorly. A daily risk limit is to prevent you from getting into a spiral of revenge trading. A good limit to stick to when starting is to stop trading if you experience three losses in a row. This is pretty unlikely with options trades to be honest, unless you screw up badly, but it's good to have a limit in place from a perspective of the discipline.

Next, aim for a maximum weekly drawdown limit of 5% and a monthly drawdown limit of 6-8%. These are pretty high limits, to be honest, and if you are a directional trader, these limits do not apply to you. Directional traders need to be a lot more conservative than options trader when it comes to risk.

Understand that these are hard stop limits. So if your account has hit its monthly drawdown level within the first week, you need to take the rest of the month off. Overtrading and a lack of reflection on progress can cause a lot of damage, and a drawdown is simply a reflection of that.

Qualitative Risk

Quantitative metrics aside, your ability to properly manage qualitative things in your life and trading will dictate a lot of your success. Prepare well, and you're likely to see progress. You need to see preparation as your responsibility. I mean, no one else can prepare for you, can they?

There are different elements to tracking your level of preparation, so let's look at them one by one.

CHAPTER - 29

MARKET TRENDS

A market is a chaotic place, with several traders vying for dominance over one another. There is a countless number of strategies and time frames in play, and at any point, it is close to impossible to determine who will emerge with the upper hand. In such an environment, how is it then possible to make any money? After all, if everything is unpredictable, how can you get your picks, right?

Well, this is where thinking in terms of probabilities comes into play. While you cannot get every single bet right, as long as you get enough right and make enough money on those to offset your losses, you will make money in the long run.

It's not about getting one or two right. It's about

executing the strategy with the best odds of winning over and over again and ensuring that your math works out with regards to the relationship between your win rate and average win.

So, it comes down to finding patterns which repeat themselves over time in the markets. What causes these patterns? Well, the other traders, of course! To put it more accurately, the orders that the other traders place in the market are what create patterns that repeat themselves over time.

The first step to understanding these patterns is to understand what trends and ranges are. Identifying them and learning to spot when they transition into one another will give you a massive leg up not only with your options trading but also with directional trading.

Trends

In theory, spotting a trend is simple enough. Look left to right, and if the price is headed up or down, it's a trend. Well, sometimes it is that simple. However, for the majority of the time, you have both with and counter-trend forces operating in the market. It is possible to have a long counter-trend reactions within a larger trend, and sometimes, depending on the time frame you're in, these counter-trend reactions take up the majority of your screen space.

Trend vs. Range

This is a chart of the UK100 CFD, which mimics the FTSE 100, on the four-hour time frame. Three-quarters of the chart is a downtrend and the last quarter is a wild uptrend. Using the looking left to the right guideline, we'd conclude that this instrument is in a range. Is that true, though?

Just looking at that chart, you can see that short-term momentum is bullish. So, if you were considering taking a trade on this, would you implement a range strategy or a trending one? This is exactly the sort of thing that catches traders up.

The key to deciphering trends is to watch for two things: counter-trend participation quality and turning points. Let's tackle counter-trend participation first.

Counter-Trend Participation

When a new trend begins, the market experiences an extremely imbalanced order flow, which is tilted towards one side. There's not much counter-trend participation against this seeming tidal wave of trend orders. Price marches on without any opposition and experiences only a few hiccups.

As time goes on, though, the with trend forces run out of steam and have to take breaks to gather themselves. This is where counter-trend traders start testing the trend and trying to see how far back into the trend they can go. While it is unrealistic to expect a full reversal at this point, the quality of the correction or pushback tells us a lot about the strength distribution between the with and counter-trend forces.

While all this is going on behind the scenes, the price chart is what records the push and pull between these two forces. Using the price chart, we can not only anticipate when a trend is coming to an end, but also how long it could potentially take before it does. This second factor, which helps us estimate the time it could take, is invaluable from an options perspective, especially if you're using a horizontal spread strategy.

In all cases, the greater the number of them, the greater the counter-trend participation in the market. The closer a trend is to end, the greater the counter-trend participation. Thus, the minute you begin to see price move into a large, sideways move with an equal number of buyers and sellers in it, you can be sure that some form of redistribution is going on.

Mind you, and the trend might continue or reverse. Either way, it doesn't matter. What matters is that you know the trend is weak and that now is probably not the time to be banking on-trend strategies.

Starting from the left, we can see that there is close to no counter-trend bars, bearish in this case, and the bulls make easy progress. Note the angle with which the bulls proceed upwards.

Then comes the first major correction, and the counter-trend players push back against the last third of the bull move. Notice how strong the bearish bars are and note their characters compared to the bullish bars.

The bulls recover and push the price higher at the original angle and without any bearish presence, which seems odd. This is soon explained as the bears' slam price back down, and for a while, it looks as if they've managed to form a V top reversal in the trend, which is an extremely rare occurrence.

The price action that follows is a more accurate reflection of the power in the market, with both bulls and bears sharing chunks of the order flow, with overall order flow in the bull's favor but only just. Price here is certainly in an uptrend, but looking at the extent of the bearish pushbacks, perhaps we should be on our guard for a bearish reversal. After all, the order flow is looking pretty sideways at this point.

So how would we approach an options strategy with the chart in the state it is in at the extreme, right? Well, for one, any strategy that requires an option beyond the near month is out of the question, given the probability of it turning. Secondly, looking at the order flow, it does seem to be following a channel, doesn't it?

While the channel isn't very clean if you were aggressive enough, you could consider deploying a collar with the strike prices above and below this channel to take advantage of the price movement. You could also employ some moderately bullish strategies as price approaches the bottom of this channel, and figuring out the extent of the bull move is easier thanks to you being able to reference the top of the channel.

As price moves in this channel, it's all well and good. Eventually, though, we know that the trend has to flip. How do we know when this happens?

Turning Points

As bulls and bears struggle over who gets to control the order flow, price swings up and down. You will notice that every time price comes back into the 6427-6349 zone, the bulls seem to step in masse and repulse the bears.

This tells us that the bulls are willing to defend this level in large numbers and strongly at that. Given the number of times the bears have tested this level, we can safely assume that above this level, bullish strength is a bit weak. However, at this level, it is as if the bulls have retreated and are treating this as a sort of last resort, for the trend to be maintained. You can see where I'm going with this.

If this level were to be breached by the bears, it is a good bet that a large number of bulls will be taken out. In martial terms, the largest army of bulls has been marshaled at this level. If this force is defeated, it is unlikely that there's going to be too much resistance to the bears below this level.

This zone, in short, is a turning point. If price breaches this zone decisively, we can safely assume that the bears have moved in and control the majority of the order flow.

Turning Point Breached

The decisive turning point zone is marked by the two horizontal lines, and the price touches this level twice more and is repulsed by the bulls. Notice how the last bounce before the level breaks produces an extremely weak bullish bounce, and price simply caves through this. Notice the strength with which the bears breakthrough.

For now, we can conclude that as long as the price remains below the turning point, we are bearishly biased. You can see this by looking at the angle with which bulls push back as well as the lack of strong bearish participation on the push upwards.

This doesn't mean we go ahead and pencil in a bull move and start implementing strategies that take advantage of the upcoming bullish move. Remember, nothing is for certain in the markets. Don't change your bias or strategy until the turning point decisively breaks.

Some key things to note here are that a turning point is always a major S/R level. It is usually a swing point where a large number of trend forces gather to support the trend. This will not always be the case, so don't make the mistake of hanging on to older turning points.

This indicates that the bears are quite strong here and that any subsequent attack will be handled the same way until the level breaks. Do we know when the level will break? Well, we can't say with any accuracy. However, we can estimate the probability of it breaking.

The latest upswing has seen very little bearish pushback, comparatively speaking, and the push into the level is strong. Instinct would say that there's one more rejection left here. However, who knows? Until the level breaks, we stay bearish. When the level breaks, we switch to the bullish side.

Putting It All Together

So now we're ready to put all of this together into one coherent package. Your analysis should always begin with determining the current state of the market. Ranges are pretty straightforward to spot, and they occur either within big pullbacks in trends or at the end of trends.

Trends vary in strength, depending on the amount of counter-trend participation they have. The way to determine counter-trend participation levels is to simply look at the price bars and compare the counter-trend ones to the trendy ones. The angle with which the trend progresses is a great gauge as well, for its strength, with steeper angles being stronger.

CONCLUSION

First of all, we would point out that the whole guide was written without relying on any kind of fee. As we already mentioned, fees vary, and every brokerage house has its own rules about it.

• Trading options have significant risks. If you are inexperienced with trading, we would recommend talking with a financial advisor before making any decision.

• Always keep in mind that every investment has its own risk and reward rating, which means that if the risk is high, the reward will be high too.

• Expiration date of American style options and European style options (the most commonly used ones) is always the third Saturday of the month for American and the last Friday before the third Saturday for European options.

• Phrase "in the money" describes that the option has a value higher than the strike price for call options and lower than the strike price for put options at the time of their expiration.

• The most common minimal bid for option sharing is one nickel or 5 dollars per contract. However, some more liquid contracts allow the minimal bid to be one dollar per contract.

• 100 shares of the certain stock are one option contract.

• If you pay 1 dollar for an option your premium for that option whether you buy or sell it is 1 dollar per share, which means that the option premium is 100 dollars per contract.

• All of the examples in this guide assume that every option order ever mentioned was filled successfully.

• Whenever you want to open a new position, you will have to sell or buy on the market to "open". The same principle applies if you wish to close your position. You sell or buy to "close."

• Phrase Open Interest represents the number of option contracts that are opened at the moment. Logically- more opened contracts mean a bigger number, and closed contracts mean a smaller number.

• Volume of the options is the number of contracts that are traded in one single day.

Be careful when signing the contracts; make sure you read all of the trading options.

They can be extremely profitable, but learning to trade them well takes time. You can choose to use indicators to determine your entry points, and I'm all for this approach at first, but remember that over the long term, you're better served learning the basics of order flow and using that.

There is no shortage of options strategies you can use to limit your risk dramatically, and depending on the volatility levels, you can deploy separate strategies to achieve the same ends. Contrast this with a directional trading strategy where you have just one method of entry, which is to either go short or go long, and only one way of managing risk, which is to use a stop loss.

Spread or market neutral trading puts you in the position of not having to care about what the market does. Besides, it brings another dimension of the market into focus, which is volatility. Volatility is the greatest thing for your gains, and options allow you to take full advantage of this, no matter what the volatility situation currently is.

Options can be a bit hard to get your head around at first since so many of us are used to looking at the market as a thing that goes up or down. Options bring a sideways and a different vertical element to it via spreads and volatility estimates. More advanced options strategies take full advantage of volatility and are more math-focused, so if this interests you, you should go for them.

That being said, do not assume the complexity means more gains. The strategies shown here are quite simple, and they will make you money thanks to the way options are structured. They bring you the advantage of leverage without having to borrow a single cent.

You can choose to borrow, of course, but you need to do this only if it is in line with your risk management math. Risk management is what will make or break your results, and at the center of quantitative risk management is your risk per trade. Keep this consistent and line up your success rate and reward to risk ratios, and you'll make money as a mathematical certainty.

Qualitative risk management requires you to adopt the right mindset with regards to trading, and you must adopt this as quickly as possible. Remember that the implications of your risk math mean that you need not be concerned with the outcome of a single trade.